Ride Gently–Ride Well

ALSO BY THE AUTHOR

The Art of Horsemanship

Ride Gently—Ride Well

By PAUL HOLMELUND

South Brunswick and New York: A. S. Barnes and Company
London: Thomas Yoseloff Ltd

A. S. Barnes and Co., Inc.
Cranbury, New Jersey 08512

Thomas Yoseloff Ltd
108 New Bond Street
London W1Y OQX, England

Second Printing, 1972

ISBN 0-498-07604-0

Printed in the United States of America

to

ANNA LEWELLEN

Contents

The Horse's Prayer

To thee, my master, I offer my prayer. Feed me, water and care for me, and when the day's work is done, provide me with shelter, a clean, dry bed and a stall wide enough for me to lie down in comfort.

Be kind to me. Talk to me. Your voice often means as much to me as the reins. Pet me sometimes, that I may serve you the more gladly and learn to love you.

Do not jerk the reins and do not whip me. Never strike, beat or kick me when I do not understand what you want. Try to understand when I do not seem to obey willingly.

Do not check me so that I cannot have the free use of my head or hurt me by pulling my head up.

Keep me well shod. Examine my teeth if I do not eat.

I may have an ulcerated and painful tooth. Do not take away my best defense against the flies and mosquitoes by cutting off my tail.

I can not tell you when I am thirsty, so give me clean cool water often.

Do not have me run on hard pavements. It makes my feet hurt and I am afraid of falling. I am strong, but do not forget that there is a limit to my strength.

And finally, O MY MASTER, when my useful strength is gone, do not turn me out to starve or freeze, or sell me to some cruel master, to be slowly tortured and starved to death.

Acknowledgments

I owe a debt of gratitude to many people and humane organizations for their advice, information and contributions. I shall mention a few of them.

THE HUMANE SOCIETY OF THE UNITED STATES is continuously proving its sincere dedication to the protection of animals, both in words and deeds.

THE NATIONAL CATHOLIC SOCIETY FOR ANIMAL WELFARE, under the leadership of Mrs. Helen E. Jones, can always be depended on when understanding and a warm heart are needed.

VIRGINIA FEDERATION OF HUMANE SOCIETIES, with Mrs. Paul M. Twyne at the helm, deserves a special vote of thanks by horse lovers for their gallant championship of the abused horse.

There are many others, like THE HUMANE SOCIETY OF LACKAWANNA COUNTY, THE MASSACHUSETTS S.P.C.A., RANCHO COASTAL HUMANE SOCIETY, PENINSULA ANIMAL WELFARE SOCIETY, that realize and try to relieve the hard lot of the horse.

There are newspapers, too, like *The Chronicle of the Horse*, that should be remembered for their generous allowance of space.

Last but not least I wish to thank INSPECTION DE L'ARME BLINDEE ET CAVALERIE, Paris, France, for the equestrian pictures shown in this book.

Introduction

The fundamental principles of good horsemanship were developed to meet the requirements of the warrior on horseback and are as valid today as they were before clanking tanks replaced the sabers.

During the golden age of horses and horsemanship there were two kinds of mounted soldiers. One of them was the mounted infantry, who used the horse only for transportation. The only demand on their equestrian ability was limited to avoid falling off during this process. The other category, the trooper, had to be an educated rider, a kind of centaur, an inseparable combination of horse and man. Imitators of the trooper and his horsemanship are not uncommon today, but their methods are crude and primitive. The educated rider on a properly trained horse performed smoothly and effortlessly, while the imitator's technique is limited to brute force.

The cavalry horse must be under complete control every moment. The cavalry man had to know that it was up to him to ride his horse actively and balance him in such a manner as to economize with his strength on a long, grinding march and have enough energy left at the end for an all-out burst of speed, without being discouraged by fences and ditches.

It should be obvious that under such circumstances the communication between horse and rider had to be something more reliable than a set of signals. It had to function without interruption. This is the key to good horsemanship. It also eliminates the constant abuse inflicted on a horse with an unschooled rider in the saddle.

Obviously, the old cavalryman's elaborate training is

out of the question for civilian riders because it would take too much time. But there is no reason why at least the fundamentals of the tested and true principles of good equitation should be replaced by half-baked conceptions, even if the schooling is limited to 30 lessons. Intelligent handling benefits both horse and rider. Understanding of the many latent talents of the horse, and how to develop and take advantage of them, makes horseback riding the most rewarding of all sports.

WHAT THE BOYS SAID

Not long ago, while walking along one of the beautiful beaches south of San Francisco, I met two boys on horseback, enjoying a morning canter. I use this expression only as a polite definition of what seems to be the modern, approved form of the more dignified style of horsemanship displayed on the bridle paths a few years ago.

These boys were galloping as fast as energetic urging could persuade the horses to go in the loose sand. That the horses were breathing heavily and audibly seemed to be taken for granted and approved of, like the satisfying thunder of a jalopy exhaust. The horses were covered with sweat, but the boys were oblivious to everything except their racing game. I persuaded them to stop and dismount for a chat. The resulting talk turned out to be quite illuminating.

To begin with, it was established that they were completely unaware of any wrong-doing. They were honestly surprised to learn that they were engaged in half killing their horses, and that for certain reasons, soft sand was not a good surface for a gallop, or for even a walk or trot. After having it explained, they readily admitted their ignorance. They also quickly saw the point when I mentioned why it was regarded as unhorseman-like to run a horse out of breath, then stop suddenly and let him stand there and recover as best he could. So we ended up by strolling back to the beach, leading the horses, while the boys argued their side.

They guessed, they said, that they had become interested in horseback riding by watching Westerns. Their admiration for straight-shooting, hard-riding heroes of the screen had led to an unshakable conviction that whatever *they* did must be right. When they saw with their own eyes how the horses tore at full speed up hill and down dale for hours and miles on end with no bad effects, it stood to reason that there could be nothing wrong with it. They challenged me to deny that these cowboy actors were the world's champion horsemen. I diplomatically ducked argument, but pointed out that the glamorous performances were mostly illusions created by photographic tricks, and that the horses actually did not run far enough or fast enough to make them breathe faster. I explained that for almost half a century the treatment of animals used in movies was under strict control of the Humane Society. The boys admitted that they did not know this, nor had anyone ever told them much about riding. All they knew for sure was how to get up into the saddle from the left side, how the reins served both as a steering wheel and brakes, that hard kicks (the harder the better) brought the same result as stepping on the gas. The proper outfit, like hats, boots and ropes, was also recognized as important.

I brought up the delicate subject of riding instruction. The reaction was a hearty belly laugh—or as close to it as good manners would permit. They had made investigations, they said, more because they were curious than because they were seriously interested. The concensus was that the instructors did not know what they were talking about. One expert would say one thing, another

would say exactly the opposite. There seemed to be no
sense in spending money on them. It is not easy to fool
teen-agers nowadays.

The boys were still young enough to possess a strong
sense of male superiority and did not yet understand the
tenets of chivalry towards the weaker sex. At any rate, they
stated quite frankly that they did not feel like taking lessons from a female teacher. Riding was a manly sport and
lady instructors were strictly for inferior creatures—like
girls.

THE DEGENERATION OF A GENTLE ART

Times have changed now. Civilization has made giant
strides forward in many respects, but good horsemanship
has been left behind. In fact, it seems to have a noticeable
tendency to move in the opposite direction, failing to keep
pace with the breeding of better and better horseflesh.
The deteriorating process starts early, practically at the
kindergarten level. It does not make sense to enter children in riding classes until they are physically and mentally ready to benefit by the instruction, usually about 14.
But at that age they are also developing a keen and critical
mind. They will no longer accept hog-wash as real instruction and very few of them can be found in the school
ring any more. Instead, the arenas of riding "academies"
are now jammed with little kids, hardly above the kindergarten age, mostly girls, having a wonderful time.

The following is a letter from a lady who had made
earnest attempts since her early teens to learn to ride
properly. She obviously became disillusioned very soon,
but not discouraged until quite recently.

I attended a riding class the other day as an observer and
can not make up my mind whether to weep or swear or
laugh.

There may be "academies," where serious-faced students ride around and around, giving silent and respectful attention to the master, whose eagle eye never misses the wrong placement of hands, feet and elbows and where the students graduate as accomplished equestriennes, who will brush off admirers with a modest laugh—"Really, you shouldn't keep asking me—I simply don't have time to join the Olympic team!"

The experience that got my dander up was different. There was nothing formal about it.

It was a class of girl scouts. As the horses were being saddled, the children were walking around freely, telling the instructor which horse they wanted to ride: "Oh, I don't want old Baldy, he won't go—!" After considerable confusion the class got going in the ring at a walk. The students sat slumped in all kinds of positions, talking and waving to each other. The instructor occasionally interrupted the gay, social atmosphere by requests to keep quiet so they could hear his commands.

Since the girls had been informed that English style riding was much too dangerous, the class was Western. The element of safety had, of course, great appeal to the mothers.

The students were allowed to hold the reins any way they wanted, and there was nothing said about the position of hands, legs and seat, or how to use these parts of the anatomy to guide the horse. The instructor sauntered over to the side of the ring to make conversation with some mothers: "Yes, Susie is doing quite well since she fell off that last time. Yes, she likes Blackie much better too." Now and then he would holler: "OK, trot!" After much kicking, whooping and waving of arms, the horses rallied from their coma and started a shuffling trot, encouraged by free use of sticks and whips.

One mother present remarked that she hated horses and that they were so dangerous, but the girls had to learn to ride properly nowadays.

As the horses ambled around the ring, the air was full of the shrieks and chatter of happy youngsters: "Mr. M., I'm bumping too much—let's stop—I don't like this horse—whee, look at me, mom—giddap—!" I am sure there was no doubt in the minds of these kids, that all horses were just like the ones they rode—no shying or bolting when they waved their arms, took their jackets off or put them back on.

After trying to control myself till I was ready to burst, I finally asked the instructor as courteously as I could, why he didn't do a little instructing. He explained that it just wasn't worth it. The kids wanted to RIDE, and he did not feel he should spoil their fun by talking about a lot of details. Besides, he said, the sessions are only so long, and unless he could keep them interested, they would quit. He was in business and could not afford to have mothers demand their money back, because their daughters got bored and refuse to complete their eight-lesson course to become expert riders. He said that children just would not stand for the strict attention to "fancy" details and discipline demanded by foreign instructors.

So, the give-and-take between instructor and students went on without serious interruptions: "When are we going to gallop—I don't like to trot—it HURTS!" Instructor: "OK, we'll gallop later when you know more." Then in an aside to the mother: "Have to be careful!" On the far side of the ring one gal got her horse running too fast and over-rode the gal in front of her: "Katie, get out of my way—can't you SEE I am coming?"

Then the instructor stops the whole class: "You MUST keep your distance—OK now Susie, back your horse—I said BACK—Oh well, just a minute, I'll move him!" By then the hour was up, the class straggles back to the stable, where they mill around, trying to dismount, getting in the way of everybody and each other.

As you know, this "academy" is not a back-woods stable. It is a fashionable establishment, in an ultra fashionable suburb, where the horse is a symbol of prestige. Heaven help the art of equitation and the poor horses.

After a few sessions like the one described by this lady, the children are supposed to have absorbed all the formal knowledge of equitation they need, except, of course, the ones who later become infected with horse-show ambitions. They will find it necessary to take a few lessons in advanced equitation, such as how to dress properly and to pose for the photographers.

All this refers to the girls and the beginning of their lives as horsewomen. Such sissy stuff is not for the boys. They get all the advice needed from Westerns. And they can always discuss technical points with their pals—in a manly way.

A few years later we will run into the same boys. They are teen-agers then and will have developed an irresistible urge for violent action, including a passion for speed and noise making. It is only natural that many of them, whose heroes are the hard-riding cowboys of screen and legend, turn to horses for excitement and glamor. They can fill the bill, both as far as speed is concerned and soul-satisfying noise. There may not be a convenient gas pedal to step on, but there are whips and glittering, clanking spurs with big wheels and spikes as sharp as needles, which look so impressive on a guy's bootheels. And what can be more downright intoxicating than the thunder of hooves on hard pavement? Or how about the panting and heaving of the critter after a full speed gallop over the hills? It just proves what a fearless rough-rider you are and that you can hold your own against Hollywood's best.

I know of a stable, within the limits of a civilized area, where anybody with the necessary cash can rent a horse and ride it (without supervision) over trails provided by the state. It is patronized by teen-agers who have no conception of how to handle a horse, and on weekends all animals are in constant use from early morning until late at night. There is a rule that the horses should be allowed 20 minutes of rest between rides. During these 20 minutes nobody has the time even to loosen the girths or remove the bridles.

All this can be classified as gross mistreatment, but it is

only of the most obvious variety. Nobody, including the unschooled horseman himself, is aware of the numerous but less obvious ways to make a horse at least very uncomfortable on a seemingly sensible ride, even during an hour or two on the trail, in polo, jumping, or cross-country riding. This is where some knowledge of the elements of good equitation is important, not least from the horse's point of view.

But what has happened in the meantime to those little girls we last heard from getting their formal education in horsemanship? Most of them will have neglected perfecting their technique in finishing schools for equestriennes, but they may still be going along with boy friends for weekend thrills on horseback. For feminine reasons that have nothing to do with the serious subjects discussed in this book, more girls than boys go in for riding in a big way—particularly horse shows. I can even remember the ladies riding side saddle in the shows, participating both in equitation classes and in jumping, performing beautifully. At that time the really serious and most interesting part of the show was the equitation and dressage classes, in which the ability of the rider as reflected by the performance of his horse was judged.

This has changed drastically over the years and today the classes in horsemanship have practically disappeared, for reasons that are only too obvious. Instead there are prizes for The Best Dressed, for Mother and Daughter Teams, and for a number of other meaningless exhibitions. Otherwise it is the horses—their conformation, action, and grooming—that are the objects of attention, both by the judges and the audience. The behavior of the riders is discreetly ignored, at least as long as they do not fall off.

More serious is the weird American phenomenon named "gaited horses," including the so-called "Tennessee Walking Horse." As far as I can gather, somebody invented them to save the tender posteriors of Southern gentlemen from the rough bumps delivered by less refined nags. They are prominent in most big shows, ambling around the tan-bark with a gait about as natural to them as a trip by pogo sticks would be to the owner.

Often, every year, somebody breaks the delicate tissues in a horse's tail and places the mangled remains in an iron bustle to be reshaped into an unsightly upright stump. Frequently the stump fails to acquire the exact angle demanded by the eagle-eyed judges, and more operations may be necessary. The painful reshaping of the tail is only part of the torture the gaited horse has to endure before he is ready to appear before the admiring public.

One of the artificial gaits is the "rack," which gives the innocent observer the impression that he is watching a new biological phenomenon, an animal with at least six legs, all moving out of step with each other as the creature tears frantically around the track.

Only the initiated know exactly what kind of hell this horse has to go through in order to change his manner of locomotion so drastically. It is, however, no secret that both mechanical and chemical processes are involved and that the initial purpose is to make his feet so sore that he gives the impression of walking on eggs.

Since the horse opera on TV seems to be budding horse-men's principal source of information as to how a he-man should handle his horse, a closer look might be important. So, next time detach your attention from the dramatic suspense for a moment and concentrate on a few technical details having to do with equitation.

You will notice how incessant, iron fisted jerks—back-wards, upwards and sideways—make the pony stop and turn and even try to rear, while its frantic efforts to avoid the torture of the bit produces the illusion of a fiery steed being controlled by a super horseman. No wonder the youngsters are impressed. Some older ones are too, judg-ing by performances in Fourth of July parades.

Students of horsemanship seldom read books on the subject, and I can hardly blame them. But magazines with pretty pictures are a different matter.

Recently the picture of a cowgirl in full western regalia, including vermilion stretchpants, appeared on the cover of a glossy magazine dealing with equestrian matters and tempted me to take a look inside. Among other things of interest to horsemen I found a story of an eight-year-old boy who, all by himself, had invented a contraption to prevent a horse from throwing his head or carrying it too high—a tie-down. It was a somewhat complex looking arrangement of chains and pieces of metal that seemed like it could break the lower jaw with little effort on the rider's part. The magazine predicted a great future for the boy as a horseman. A Humane officer friend of mine, however, stated flatly that he would arrest anybody caught using the invention in his territory.

With the exception of individual cases of brutality and ignorance, most cases of serious abuse are to be found behind the scenes. Certain features of breaking and training methods are hidden from public view, for very good reasons. I still have nightmares involving the breaking of a colt, Western style, which it was my misfortune to attend. It must be admitted that it was highly efficient and time-saving. It all took less than one week, but when it was over, that young pony was really "broke," in spirit that is. It just stood there, spraddle-legged, glassy eyed, head hanging.

After three days of recovery it was safe to ride and could be put to work. As the trainer said, all the orneriness (some of us call it "joie de vivre") had been knocked out of it. The operators of the horse-training business are surrounded by a certain aura of mystery. But there is sound reasoning behind their recent appearance in rapidly increasing numbers. The disappearance of bona fide riding instructors created a vacuum. Since nobody could be found to teach the riders how to take care of the horses, the logical solution was to train the horses so they could take care of the riders.

This system had the advantage that it no longer would be necessary to waste time and money on tiresome riding lessons. Even if the horse should become confused after a while and unable to perform as it was expected of him due to the fumbling ineptness of his rider, he could always be sent back to the trainer for reconditioning. I was present recently when one young lady brought her horse back for that purpose. She said it was getting dopey, had no pep and was dragging its feet. Smiling knowingly and reassuringly, the trainer patted the young lady's arm: "Don't worry. A little spur-and-whip treatment will snap him out of it—call for him day after tomorrow." This trainer was a member of the gentle sex.

Yes, horse training is a goldmine, and interested parties lost no time getting in on the bonanza. In 1963 *The Saturday Evening Post* told about an appeal to Congress by the representative from Montana for permission to import a horse trainer from Australia. In spite of energetic efforts it had proved impossible to find a qualified American.

It should be of interest to have revealed where the suddenly appearing army of presumed experts got their diplomas, particularly since they are setting themselves up as authorities, not only as horse trainers, but on equestrian matters as well.

Conditions like these ought to justify my attempt to offer some advice, although it is unsolicited, about how to derive real value from horseback riding, and at the same time make life a little easier for our horses.

Ride Gently–Ride Well

PART I

What Every Horseman Should Know

"Out of a thousand centuries
they drew the ancient
admiration of the footman
for the horseman. They knew
instinctively that a man on
a horse is spiritually as
well as physically bigger
than a man on foot."
John Steinbeck.

1. Mounting and Dismounting

In good horsemanship there are no details so unimportant that they can be ignored. They have all been studied carefully and they are based on practical common sense. Since there can be a real element of danger connected with this process, I feel the matter deserves some unfavorable attention, at least where children are concerned. For this reason I feel justified in quoting instructions contained in an official booklet published in 1958 for the guidance of children. There is an illustration that shows a boy standing beside a horse, facing mostly forward, and so far back that the entire saddle appears to be in front of him. He is, in other words, in an ideal position for the horse to reach him with a side swipe of his left hind leg—a common way to discourage the rider from mounting. From personal experience I can testify to one case where a man received a broken leg in exactly that manner.

One can not help wondering, either, what will happen if the horse should decide to start walking at this awkward moment. Few horses are so well behaved that they will remain immobile while a rider goes through the motions of mounting.

The picture further shows the boy with all four (slack) reins in his *right* fist, holding on to the pommel with the same hand. When we consider that the girth may not be as tight as it should be, that the saddle may be dislodged even by a slight pull and that the reins must be transferred to the left hand, it seems that this is going to be a very busy scout during the next few seconds, even if he avoids being kicked or displacing the saddle.

As if all this were not enough, he is holding the stirrup

in his *left* hand. At this stage he does not have time to fiddle, but in one fluent motion he must:

1. Insert his foot in the stirrup.
2. Turn toward the horse.
3. Transfer four reins to his left hand.
4. Prevent the horse from walking away from him (with the reins hanging loose).

His contortions from then on are somewhat blurred, and I can only quote what the book says:

1. Prepare to mount. *Eyes front,* reins evenly in right hand, turn stirrup sideways.
2. At count of one: right hand on pommel, *eyes front,* stirrup on *ball of foot,* heel down, lower leg vertical, reins collected.
3. At the count of two: weight on extended arms, body across pommel, reins still level.
4. At the count of three: it's all aboard. Reins collected and level, back slightly hollow, *eyes front,* hands neat (!), stirrups vertical. Heels could be slightly lower!

It may appear from the above that I am trying to be humorous, but I can see nothing funny in distortion of common sense, particularly when the safety of youngsters is involved. Horsemen who took equitation more seriously will now agree that the easiest and most practical way to mount is as follows:

1. Stand close to the horse's shoulder, facing toward his tail. Gather all four reins in the left hand—snaffle reins tight, curb reins loose, the horse's head slightly flexed to the right. Take a firm grip on the withers (not on the pommel) with the left hand. The stirrup is gripped by the right hand, left foot inserted from the outside, all the way in to the heel. In this position, the horse will not get away from you by stepping forward. If he does, he

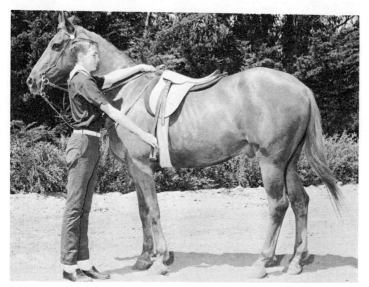

"Prepare to mount."

will actually help you to get up and into the saddle. Some horses may try to back up to escape you, but can easily be discouraged by being forced backwards a step or two. Standing by the shoulder you are safe from being kicked, and the shortened right snaffle prevents the horse from circling around you, as well as from nipping you in the seat of the pants with his teeth.

2. Make a half turn to the left, still as close to the horse as possible, press the left knee against his flank, reach across the saddle with your right hand and take a light hold of the cantle.

3. Jump off on the ball of your right foot and use your hand on the withers to help the jump with a pull. Stop there, leaning with your full weight on straight arms, not on the left foot in the stirrup.

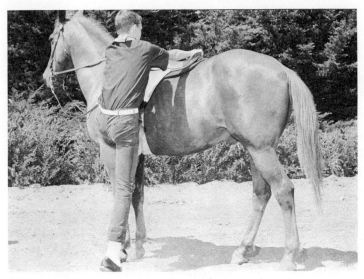

"Mount."

4. Transfer your weight to the left arm, swing the right leg as high over the croup as you can (while the right hand slides forward into a supporting position on the pommel) and settle down in the saddle slowly and lightly. Be careful not to lose your balance while you are swinging your leg over or leaning on your arms on the pommel. An accidental jerk on the reins or a heavy bump into the saddle at that moment may start serious trouble.

Movements 2, 3 and 4 should develop into one fluent motion.

Little attention is as a rule paid to how you get off a horse and quite a few students of equitation have to find out the hard way why it may be a good idea to do it correctly. Just a few days ago I happened to witness a dignified young equestrienne being up-ended in the process of climbing off her horse. Fortunately there was

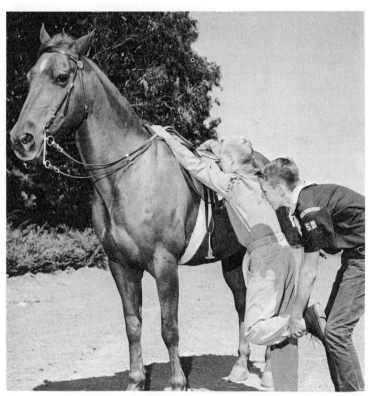

A Helping Hand.

no damage except to her feelings, but there easily could
have been. She was caught with one foot on the ground
and the other in the stirrup, when the horse decided
to walk away. She forgot to keep a hold on the reins,
too. The most sensible technique of dismounting is as
follows: Take all reins in the left hand, which is planted
firmly on the withers. Take the right foot out of the stirrup, lean on both arms (with the right hand on the pommel) and swing the right leg over the croup. Move the

right hand at the same time from the pommel to the seat of the saddle, lean on your arms and remove the left foot from the stirrup before sliding down.

The disadvantage of the more informal way of dismounting is that the reins must be transferred to the right hand during the operation, which consists of lifting the right leg across the horse's neck. Whatever system is used, do not forget to have both feet clear of the stirrups before starting down.

2. Building the Foundation

It stands to reason that a beginner never should be put aboard a horse that is not safe and gentle. But the purpose of education in horsemanship should always be to learn how to handle and control horses that have not been "whip-trained" into a condition of dull and lifeless resignation by some trainer. There is no greater pleasure in equitation than the feeling of being in complete control and harmony of a high-spirited fine horse.

The first step in learning to ride is to acquire a seat in the saddle that can not be dislodged as long as the horse is on his legs.

This safety in the saddle can only be based on suppleness and balance. A convulsive grip with the legs will only make matters worse when the going gets rough, and it will inevitably lead to a disgraceful climax. To use the reins as a life line, to depend on the stirrups or to try the horn of a Western saddle as an emergency anchor will be found to be equally disastrous. Youngsters should be allowed to ride without stirrups as long as time will allow, and while they are walking or trotting around the school ring, the reins should be tied up and left hanging on the horse's neck or withers. The students should sit completely relaxed, with their shoulders loose and their arms folded or behind their backs. A little twisting and bending helps to relax joints and muscles. Lifting a leg at a time across to the other side and "falling off"—either by simply sliding down or by grabbing the horse firmly around the neck with both arms, swinging the right leg over the croup, then stretching both legs together, with straight knees and retaining the grip around the neck till the feet touch the ground—will help a lot to build confidence.

While gripping with the legs for safety must be discouraged, the legs should not be allowed to hang completely loose. At a very early stage the student should learn and develop a habit—to keep the flat inner side of his thighs against the saddle by taking hold (with his hands) of the thick muscle in his upper leg and pull it back, away from the saddle.

Relaxed and depending on his balance, the student must learn to adjust himself to the movements of his horse, regardless of how rough they may be, to roll with the punches and avoid the effects of the bumps by sitting down on them instead of straining away from them. He will soon find out that his only salvation from severe punishment is to try to imitate a dishrag, leaning back and sagging in a round-shouldered position. This is, however, only a temporary remedy. Active suppleness must gradually replace passive relaxation, the sagging backbone must be straightened and pulled slightly in, the shoulders adjusted into a more graceful position.

Balance as well as muscle action will increasingly develop from purely instinctive responses into controlled reactions, governed by the rider's growing sensitiveness of feel. Preparing for a turn, for instance, he will transfer his center of gravity toward the new direction. He must learn to do so by sliding his seat a trifle in the saddle instead of bending from the waist.

Whenever something unexpected happens, if something frightens the horse, for instance, the rider will instinctively tighten up muscles, nerves and everything. By doing so, he transmits his panic to the horse, who may then really get out of hand. Furthermore, by tying himself up in a knot, he makes it very easy for the horse to get rid of him. This is only one occasion that illustrates how important it is to know how to relax at will, both mentally and physically. A horse always knows when the rider is scared and reacts to it, but the horse usually gets the blame. A clumsy and unstable seat or unsteady balance is enough to provoke a spirited horse, till he gets out of control. A stiff, clumsy and precariously balanced rider means severe punishment also to the poor nags who have had all resistance beaten out of them. A greenhorn rider of this type is not only annoying, but actually a heavier burden to a horse than a good rider of twice his weight. Most saddle sores are caused by riders who bump the horse in the back with every step he takes and who move around incessantly in the saddle, from side to side, from pommel to cantle.

A poorly balanced rider has little or no control of his hands. Every time he bounces, he will jerk on the reins. Every time he feels wobbly he will do the same. Considering the fact that a horse's gums are just as sensitive as our own and not protected by teeth where the bit rests against them, it should not be hard to understand why fingers and hands should be so sensitive and steady that the rider should be able to hold a glass of water, filled to the brim, and ride in all gaits without spilling a drop.

THE POSITION

The cornerstones of the rider's position in the saddle are the points of contact that make it possible to control the horse. The seat of his pants, supporting his weight, must be placed where full advantage can be taken of the effect of 170 pounds of regulating pressure. The legs below the knees, with their tensed muscles, must be in easy, constant and effective contact with the horse's ribs. And, finally, the hands must be placed and adjusted to make a sensitive, elastic and live shock-absorbing link between the horse's mouth and the rider's arms.

Inside the framework of the aids, the rest of the rider's

Excellent position: seat well forward in the saddle; thighs and knees flat against saddle, indicated by slightly turned-out sole; heel down, tensing calf muscle in effective contact with horse's flank.

position can then be constructed, in conformity with the laws of balance, grace and comfort.

Unfortunately, the average person's anatomy is rarely shaped to fit the saddle properly without considerable adjustment, which involves some wrenching and straightening and bending, a certain amount of painful effort, that can not be expected to arouse much enthusiasm among the pushbutton set. The regrettable results are only too obvious where people appear on horseback.

THE SEAT

Experts are forever discussing "the forward seat," "the jumping seat," "the park seat," "the show seat," and probably half a dozen other "seats" that were lately invented to satisfy the hunger for something new. Presuming that all this refers to "position," it seems to me that common sense and the laws of nature would automatically solve the problem.

The first consideration is to place rider's weight where the horse can support it with the least effort, on the least vulnerable part of his back. This area is immediately behind the withers. This is also where the rider is in the best position both to control and to balance himself as well as his horse.

The weakest part of the horse's back is under and behind the cantle (which is worth remembering also when mounting). The horse may already have his back up after a hard-fisted saddling process, and a heavy and clumsy landing of 170 pounds on top of it may start some serious trouble. Besides, the kidneys are right under the small of the horse's back and a prolonged pounding on these parts will sooner or later result in serious ailments.

With the saddle correctly placed, there should always be a hand's breadth of open space in the saddle behind the rider's seat.

There is always a tendency to slide back when sitting the trot or canter and even at a walk. The rider should constantly be aware of this and develop an unconscious habit of using the motions of the horse to counteract the backsliding.

It is of the utmost importance that the rider "follows" his horse. This means he must assume a slightly forward-leaning position when the horse is advancing normally. A heavy driving seat must, however, be applied on a balky horse, during collecting exercises, parades and pirouettes; in short, whenever the horse is required to transfer more of his weight to his hindquarters. Increased pressure of a heavy seat on one side of the saddle only becomes important when starting the canter or changing direction, for example.

A common but bad fundamental position: hands too high, seat too far back, legs sticking forward.

The preceding position corrected.

The meaning of the word "seat" has become somewhat vague in equitation parlance. It is not an exact definition like the French "assiette," but it includes all of the rider's anatomy from head to heel. However, there used to be a class at horse shows called "Hands and Seat Class," which seems to indicate that the hands were regarded as a separate unit. From the informed rider's point of view, the importance of the seat is two-fold: the adjustment of the upper body for balance and the regulation of pressure on the seat knuckles, both as to strength and direction.

A light seat in dressage and the school ring (used, for instance, in backing) is obtained by leaning slightly forward and at the same time pulling the small of the back in. While this adjustment of the seat is hardly noticeable in school riding, it becomes more obvious when jumping, going up a steep incline or sliding downhill. All pressure is then removed from the seat and transferred to thighs, knees and stirrups by leaning more strongly forward.

A stiffening of the back muscles, accompanied on occasion by a tendency to lean slightly back, will result in the heavy seat, used when slowing or stopping and also to balance the horse on his hindquarters.

Equally important is the sensitive transfer of weight from one side of the saddle to the other. As we shall see later, this is necessary, not only to avoid falling off in a turn, but also to inform the horse of what is wanted of him and help him to balance himself for a change of direction or for starting canter with the desired lead.

Not so long ago I had the privilege of watching a class in horsemanship at a very exclusive club in California. The class consisted of teen-age girls in boots, breeches and bowler hats. The instructor was downright majestic in manners and personality. The horses were fat, shiny and dull. I had my notebook and pencil ready, but found no use for them. Besides "On the Wall, At the trot, At the canter, At the walk," all that imposing teacher said by way of instruction was "Sit straight," repeated more or less regularly during one solid hour.

It so happens that a position in the saddle that is correct in every detail for purely practical reasons is also the most graceful. There are no hunched shoulders or no flapping elbows because the upper arms must be held against the body in order to make steady hands possible. There are no loosely rolling legs with knees and toes pointing out. There are no hands holding the reins awkwardly.

There is no military stiffness in a good position, but there must never be any sign of sloppyness. Ignorance of good horsemanship can not be covered up by bluff or pretended nonchalance, even when such elementary stuff as just sitting on a horse is concerned.

THE LEGS

Out West it is an accepted fact that the accomplished horseman, regardless of whether he spends his entire life or only weekends in the saddle, should be bowlegged and walk as if he were coming down a hill. This is taken to be proof of much hard riding with the legs wrapped around the horse like a plumber's tongs gripping a drain pipe. This conception clashed with the cavalry man's credo that an old trooper should show signs of being knock-kneed. In an attempt to solve the problem I decided to ride with some working cowboys down in Texas for a while. The outcome was that, considering their type of work and the special kind of saddle used, I had to admit that the long stirrups had a distinct advantage and that the resulting bowlegs should be regarded with respect. This does not mean that they are practical also for pleasure riding, even if Western equipment is used. I shall attempt to explain why.

A slight adjustment is necessary to make a beginner fit the "English" saddle, mainly due to stiff hip joints and a heavy thigh muscle. A firm seat requires that both the knee and the flat inside surface of the thigh are snug against the saddle. Exercises to insure the firm and effortless grip with thighs and knees consist of pulling the thick muscle out of the way by hand or swinging one leg at a time, with a straight knee and muscles relaxed, forward—out—back against the saddle and forward again.

Beginners who are inclined to use the stirrups for support will have a tendency to ride with them too short and the knees too high. As a result, the seat will be pushed too far back and the boots will become practically useless as an aid because they can not make contact in the right place. I have always wondered how a jockey manages to "boot" his horse home. Too long stirrups will, of course, have equally disastrous effects, in a different way, on both seat and boots as means of control. No general rule can be established as to the correct length of the stirrups. The shape and size of legs vary too much. Some are long and thin, some are short and fat. The problem must be solved for each individual case.

The conformation of the horse is also a deciding factor. The important consideration is that the boots should make effortless contact with the horse's flanks immediately behind the girth.

The rider's weight applied through his seat is always the fundamental means of control. The boots are no less important instruments of communication between horse and rider. As soon as the position of the knees has been established, as well as the length of the stirrups, the boots should connect with their points of contact by bending the knees naturally. The toes will then point forward and slightly out. They should under no circumstances be forced into an unnatural direction. Most beginners have a tendency to pull their heels up before they learn to relax. This may turn into an unfortunate habit and should be attended to from the start.

By pressing the heel down lower than the toe, the muscle in the calf is stretched and becomes hard. It is this knot of hard muscle that is needed to convey our commands to the horse by way of his flank and make the boot effective. Another reason for "heels down" is to prevent accidents when the time comes to wear spurs. Full flexibility of the ankles must be preserved.

Except in fast and difficult riding outside the arena, when it is adviseable to insert the foot in the stirrup to the heel, the point of support should be the ball of the foot—not the toe. The stirrup usually being considerably wider than the foot, the toe of the boot should be kept mainly on the part of the foot rest nearest the horse, on the heel of the big toe. The result will be a tendency to turn the sole of the boot away from the horse and permit a firmer grip with the knees.

HANDS AND REINS

In spite of the fact that hands and fingers are far from being inactive, their function is nevertheless of a more passive nature than the action of the two other aids, seat, and boots. Their job is of a more regulating and adjusting nature. Animated by seat and boots, the horse is restrained by reins and bit. The bit is never pulled back on the horse; the horse is urged against the bit but prevented from leaning on it because a constant, gentle play with the fingers on the reins keeps it alive and moving.

A high degree of sensitiveness of touch is demanded of the hands, and it is important that a position permitting full liberty of movement both of wrists and fingers is given the most careful attention.

Complete control of the hands is possible only when the student no longer needs to worry about losing his balance or being disturbed by the horse's motions. The development of good hands is frequently the most difficult part of the horseman's training. Their position must be such that a constant, sensitive and always elastic connection is maintained between the rider's hands and the horse's mouth. It is a delicate link of communication and must never degenerate into becoming an instrument to enforce obedience by brute strength.

The position of the hands, accepted as the most practical, combining steadiness with sensitive suppleness, is as follows: with upper arms and elbows resting loosely against the body, the hands are closed lightly on the reins, on edge, with the thumbs uppermost, immediately in front of the pommel and an inch or two above the withers. The upper arms against the body help to steady the hands and permit free, controlled play in the wrists. If the backs of the hands are allowed to turn up, the elbows will stick out and the action of the hands becomes erratic and rough.

In their correct position, the hands should be bent slightly toward each other, allowing easy flexibility. They shall be so close together that the reins touch the neck on both sides. A good horseman's hands and fingers are constantly alive, more or less like a violin virtuoso's. The purpose is two-fold: to avoid jerks and to keep the bit playing gently in the horse's mouth. A frozen hand and a dead bit mean disrupted communication between horse and rider.

The standard position of the hands must be adjusted to obey the demands of varying conditions. When the rider is leaning forward, jumping or passing over rough terrain, the hands should be well forward, pressed down and close together on the horse's neck; the grip of the fingers should be slightly loosened, allowing the reins to slide between them. Leaning firmly on the hands in this position will prevent them from flying up and the rider from losing his balance. The position of the hands may also have to be adjusted to counteract deviations in the position of the horse's head. If he carries it too high, the hands will be a little lower, but never below the withers. The hands may have to come up if the head is too low and accompanied by boring on the bit.

When a snaffle bit with a single rein is used, one rein is held in each hand. Both hands are needed for proper control of the horse. The nonchalant one-hand technique will sooner or later result in a twisted position. In order to get the most secure grip on them, the single rein runs from the bit into the hands between the ring fingers and the little fingers and up through the hands. It comes out across the second joint of the index fingers, where the thumbs clamp down on them and prevent slipping, while the other fingers are then left free to play the reins. Clutching the reins with the whole fist firmly closed must for obvious reasons be avoided.

When a snaffle is combined with a curb and two pairs of reins are used, they should still be carried in both hands, except on certain formal occasions that rarely, if ever, occur nowadays. In case such an occasion should arise, this is the way it is done: The left hand, in the position previously described, is held directly above the withers. The left snaffle rein runs into the hand outside the little finger; one curb rein on each side of the third finger; the right snaffle between middle and index fingers; all of them come up together through the hand and are kept in place by the thumb across the second joint of the index finger.

For quiet riding on the trail I personally prefer to carry all four reins in my left hand. The right hand is then free to do minor adjustments of the curb reins and prevent them from becoming too tight. A more cautious way is to keep the right snaffle separated in the right hand, which then can still be used to regulate the other reins.

For fast riding or jumping, using two reins in each hand is recommended, one on each side of the ring finger, the snaffle rein always on the outside.

There are various common-sense reasons for holding the reins according to accepted rules. A better and more secure grip is, for instance, obtained by having the single rein run into the hand between little finger and third finger, rather than using the full-hand grip where the rein enters the hand outside the little finger. When riding with two reins in each hand they are for the same reason held on each side of the third finger instead of the little finger.

A good hand first depends on how the reins are held, second on how they are used. A secure grip is required, but it must not interfere with sensitive handling, including constant attention to delicate adjustments.

3. Active Riding

The saddle is no place to indulge in *dolce far niente*. Button pushers should limit their activities to effort-saving mechanical toys. An up-to-date rider seems to demand a horse that needs no urging and a minimum of guiding. He does not want a nag that he has to kick every step out of. What he wants is a fiery steed (in appearance), a lamb in lion's clothing, trained to such perfection that it can take care of him and see to it that he comes to no harm.

This type of horseman will miss the greatest pleasure equitation has to offer: the feeling of complete control and the willing, spontaneous response of a happy horse. To obtain control a rider must take advantage of every point of contact he has with his horse. Most important of all is the development of "feel"—feel of balance, feel in hands and finger tips, feel in seat to regulate pressure, feel in calf muscles. A good horseman is even expected to have such delicate feel in the point of his spurs that he at all times can sense whether he is touching the horse's hide or merely ruffling the hair.

In spite of such obvious facts, I learned the other day that the instructor at a prominent girls' school explained to the young ladies that their boots or jodhpurs must never show signs of having touched the horse. As far as I could gather, it had something to do with the elegance of the position in the saddle.

To the well-educated rider the aids are not only the means by which he can control tempo, gait and direction. They also make it possible to regulate the horse's action, eliminate unnecessary effort and improve his endurance without abusing him, both by developing his muscle system and by showing him how to work in a more economical manner.

Too many would-be horsemen feel it is too much trouble even to pay attention to the hands, besides holding on to the reins in any old way. How to hold them, much less how to use them, looks too much like work—mental and otherwise. It seems a bit strange that such fanatical observance of detail is regarded as necessary when playing golf, tennis and ball games, but it is looked upon as fancy fiddle-faddle—all right for the kids to fool with, but beneath a man's dignity—in riding. It becomes tiresome, too, to sit in the same position in the saddle for any period of time. Comfort demands changes of position once in a while.

From a passenger's point of view, objections like these are justified, but nevertheless regrettable. Conditions have never before been as favorable for horseback riding as they are today, and it is a pity and a shame that fewer and fewer people know how to get the full enjoyment from it. The result is an ugly waste of good horseflesh, mistreatment and abuse. But as long as these people are honestly convinced that they are missing nothing, there is not much anybody can do to improve conditions.

It takes a long time and consistent practice to create full cooperation between horse and rider and this becomes possible only when sensitive feel and constant attention begin to replace mechanical movements.

Contact with the horse through the medium of the aids is necessary also from a psychological point of view. It affects his instinctive attitude toward his master; it is like holding a child's hand in the dark. If he has once learned to accept and to depend on the guidance of seat, boots and reins, the danger of his getting out of hand because he is frightened or nervous is no longer a cause of worry. If the contact, even for short periods, is interrupted, a well-trained horse will immediately feel insecure and uneasy. But it is imperative that the horse, particularly a sensitive one, is aware of the rider's control at all times, which is why bit and boot must be alive. Obviously, a horse can not be expected to obey the action of the aids unless he understands what it means. This can be accomplished only by patient and expert training.

In addition to remaining "alive" in order to keep the horse's attention, the three main aids are as a rule never used separately but in coordination. A good horseman is riding with his entire body. If the bit stops playing, the horse forgets it, stops chewing on it and starts leaning on it. The flexibility of jaw and neck is lost and he becomes sluggish and heavy in the hand; his entire balance changes. The same principle applies to the boots. Awareness of their gentle tapping makes control possible without the use of spurs.

The correct application of the boots, unfortunately, feels like hard work to the beginner and is one reason why modern youngsters never learn to ride properly. It takes time and effort to train the leg muscles for efficient use in the saddle.

The inactive rider misses completely the real exhilaration of horseback riding. All he gets is transportation. He is a dead weight and a heavy burden to his horse. A good rider uses the muscles of his back and loins constantly, not only to follow his motions, but to stimulate and animate him to make his work both easier and more efficient.

Properly guided, a horse under saddle would seem to the observer to be performing without the benefit of the rider's influence. Even the most complicated movements appear to be executed without visible effort by the rider. In fact, the general impression is that the horse has been taught by some anonymous trainer to do certain things, and that all the rider has to do is to stay in the saddle, maybe giving the animal a mysterious signal from time to time. It is quite true, that a well-trained horse will perform with little effort on the rider's part, but he can not do it unless the rider knows his stuff too.

FLEXING

Flexing is a fundamental requirement under all conditions of equitation; in fact, it is the key to effective control of the saddle horse and should be introduced to the student at an early stage of his education. It should be explained that it is not enough to control a horse's head. It can, for instance, be difficult to stop a horse if he stretches or stiffens his neck or points his nose to the sky. But if his neck and jaw are flexed and his head is in the right position, a pull on the reins will be transmitted through the rider's seat to the hindlegs. In other words, a pull on the reins should be transmitted from the horse's mouth,

Flexing overdone. Horse's head should be raised by sharp snap with right snaffle rein, not curb.

through the rider's seat to the hindlegs. A horse with a dead mouth, a stiff jaw, and neck, can not be schooled and is potentially dangerous.

Without flexing, the horse will take most of the weight under saddle, including his own, on his frontlegs. This will drastically reduce his endurance and increase his vulnerability to harm and abuse. For protection he must be ridden in such a way that back and hindquarters are taking more of the weight. This is of the greatest importance on long rides. To a horseman it is disgusting to see a Sunday rider trotting or cantering with the reins long and dangling. The only occasion when the reins are loose on the trail is during the intervals of rest and relaxation.

A horse that is well ridden always has an arched neck. This improves his appearance, but there are more important reasons for it.

When introduced to the flexing the beginner should be standing in front of his horse with his thumbs through the rings of the snaffle bit; he should play the bit gently until the horse begins to chew on it. When he does that his jaw will be loose and his head can be bent back, arching the neck. He is next made to flex left and right, while attention is called to the muscle along the crest slipping over to the side of the bend. The neck must be kept straight during this exercise and the head perpendicular. When the flexing is next practiced from the saddle, the boots must prevent the horse from backing.

ADVANCING

As time goes on, the techniques of equitation become less and less complicated. To the "Instant Horsemen" of the push-button era, a kick in the ribs means "go" and a jerk on the reins means "stop." It is not to be expected that the more involved operation favored by the old fogies would have a chance to be even seriously considered any more, in spite of several points in its favor, but it can do no harm to mention how we used to do it.

To set the horse in motion, for instance, the first move was to increase the pressure of the seat by a stiffening of the back. Simultaneous tapping with the boots provided added animation. The horse got the idea, but was gently prevented from advancing till he had pulled his hindlegs under him. The purpose of this preparation was to collect him. It was required that the advance from the spot should start with a front leg. This sounds plain silly, but it is one of those details that becomes increasingly important in more advanced equitation.

With the horse properly prepared, the signal to start moving consisted of a slight loosening of the reins, like letting a bird fly out of your hand.

FULL PARADE

This does not mean what you think. It is an old-fashioned expression signifying stepping on the brakes and it is nothing but a sissified version of the more heroic method as demonstrated in Westerns on the screen, where jawbreaker bits and the hero's manly strength produces more spectacular results.

As could be expected, the start of the parade did not seem to make much sense. In fact, the rider began to act as if he wanted to go faster instead of stopping. He would dig his seat knuckles down in the saddle the way he did when he wanted to advance. On top of that, he increased the animation with his boots (tapping, not kicking). But as soon as the horse thought he was invited to move faster, the bit took over with repeated, gentle pulls, proving to be more convincing than seat and boots. The horse had to stop, and since this came more or less as a surprise to him, he stopped "at attention," with his hindlegs well under him, which was exactly what the rider wanted. He had

come to a halt collected and ready to advance, turn or
back up without going through the act of a sleepy dog
getting up from his rug.

It must be kept in mind that we are still referring to the
beginner and that all these fancy antics will mean nothing
to him until later.

WALKING

Proceeding at a walk, the green student would get another unpleasant shock. Heaving a sigh of relief, he prepared to settle down to enjoy a leisurely ride, letting the
horse do the work, when teacher rudely jerked him out
of his pleasant illusion and left no doubt that the riding
ring was not going to be a place for day-dreaming and
enjoyment of informal conversation. He was actually invited, in no uncertain terms, to settle down to something
that sounded like an unrelenting grind with no end or
relief in sight. Since any element of "fun" seemed to be
missing, the deal would hardly have been acceptable to
the modern teen-age auto mechanic. But the prevailing
school of thought at that time was that anything worth
doing was worth doing well, so we had to accept the in-
evitable, whether we liked it or not. We found out ten
years later that it was very fortunate for us that we had
no vote in the matter. We would have missed all the real
enjoyment of riding. Even at a leisurely walk we were
kept busy. No slouching was allowed. We had to keep our
lower legs, the boots, active all the time, tapping away
against the horse's ribs, until our legs felt ready to drop
off. Later, when our leg muscles got stronger, we learned
the more effortless way of rhythmical taps, making contact with left and right boot alternately, in step with the
horse. We soon found that they would swing that way
practically by themselves. The right boot would tap at
the moment when the right hindleg was off the ground,

moving forward, for instance; then the same on the left side. This created a minor muscle reflex in the horse's flank and hindleg that would carry this an extra inch or two forward.

In the meantime, steady connection was maintained with the horse's mouth by constantly playing the bit and keeping it alive, with the reins held well out toward the finger tips, wrists flexed.

TROT AND CANTER

At the faster gaits—trot and canter—the use of the aids follow the same principles, although their coordination and adjustment to varying circumstances will depend more on the rider's feel. Starting the canter from the trot, for instance, if a heavy seat has been used, feel alone can be the guide in smooth execution.

At the trot, except when posting, the boots are used the same way as at a walk, tapping at the moment when the hindleg on the same side is off the ground and starts to move forward. At the canter the rhythmical application, in step with the horse's movements, is also the most effective stimulation, except that the boots then make contact simultaneously at the exact moment when the rider's weight comes down more heavily as the front feet hit the ground. The hindfeet will at that instant be in the air and the reflex created by the sharp tap of the boots will make the hindlegs reach forward an extra inch or two.

4. Schooling Movements

The full parade (pulling in from a walk, trot or canter to a halt) is a severe test of the rider's ability as well as the horse's discipline, varying with the tempo and gait at which it is executed.

The popular strong-arm method of performing this seemingly simple action has unfortunately become one of the most common and disgusting forms of abuse.

THE SHORT TURN

This is a turn on the spot, with one frontleg as a stationary pivot. To make the picture clear, let us look at a short turn to the left, the hindquarters moving to the left around the RIGHT front leg.

The first step is to increase the pressure of the seat on the right side of the saddle. Then the boot on the same side is brought into action with short, sharp taps a trifle behind its normal position. The horse's head must not be turned or flexed to either side. He must not be allowed to take more than one step at a time, under full control. The left boot must be on guard and ready to prevent him from spinning around like a top. Both boots must be alert and active to discourage any tendency to step backward. The horse is required to be on the bit during the entire movement. He will also be inclined to walk away over his left shoulder. Indirect action by the left rein should prevent this.

THE TWO-TRACK

The principle of the two-track is to walk or trot the horse in a slightly sideways position, the hindquarters following a track slightly to the left or the right of the forehand. The short turn should be used as a preparation for this movement.

There are various forms of two-track. The simplest form is when the horse moves with his neck and body straight. It can also be executed with the neck and jaw flexed and the body bent, resulting in more complicated movements that are valuable as preparations for the start of canter in dressage by balancing the horse over the proper hindleg. In its simplest form it is an effective means of developing obedience and suppleness.

In order to clarify the picture let us suppose you are riding in the regulation square ring with your left side toward the center. You want to push your horse's hindquarters out toward the fence. The easiest way is to start the two-track when passing a corner leading to the long side of the arena. Continue the curve and wheel the horse's forehand a foot or two inside the track. When this point is reached, increase the pressure of your seat on the left side of the saddle and apply the left boot a trifle further back than the right in quick, sharp stabs. Flex the horse's head, immediately behind the jaw, slightly to the left by direct action of the left rein. Prevent the right shoulder from slipping back on the track by indirect action of the right rein. At the same time the right boot must also be active, in a position distinctly further forward than the left, to prevent the horse from slowing down or stopping.

The oblique position should never be exaggerated because it makes it more difficult for the horse to move and serves no good purpose. The rider should be satisfied as soon as the willing response of the horse results in a slightly limping gait. The beat and the free elastic action must always be maintained.

If the two-track is to be executed with the hindquarters inside the track, away from the fence, riding in the same direction as before, the weight is transferred to the right side of the saddle, supporting the right boot. In this case the easiest way is also to start in passing a corner. Just before completing the turn the horse is in the right position. Stop the turn right there by indirect action of the left rein, flex his head slightly to the right, and proceed as explained before, with the application of the aids reversed.

The two-track should be kept up for only a few beats at a time and at a reduced tempo, whether the gait is walk or trot.

Two-track is never practiced at a canter.

VOLTES AND TURNS

We have so far discussed only the principles of how the horse is controlled when moving on a straight line. Guiding him properly in a turn is somewhat more complicated. Practice consists in turning in from one of the long sides of the arena, heading across in a straight line and, upon reaching the other side, either turning in the same direction or changing hands. A small volte is executed by turning in from one of the long sides, circling and returning to the track at the same spot where the circle started, or leaving the half-finished circle at a tangent and returning to the track in the opposite direction. As a practice in control, it is required that the circle is the exact size desired, that it is an exact circle, and that the tempo during the entire movement remains unbroken.

During the turn, the horse's body from nose to tail should be bent in an arc, completely covering the arc of the turn. In other words, the hindlegs should follow exactly in the tracks of the front feet.

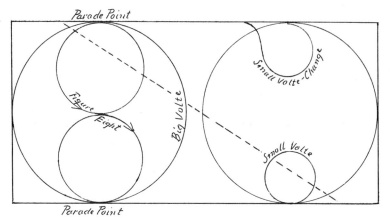

School Arena.

Sliding the seat slightly to the inside by pressing down
in the heel on that side will give the horse the first warning of what is expected of him. The outside boot is then
moved an inch or two back from normal and made itself
felt in order to prevent the hind quarters from swinging
out. The inside boot will have to be more animating in
order to maintain the tempo, while the inside rein points
the head in the new direction. The outside hand moves
up above the inside with the rein pushing against the neck
to force the shoulders into the turn. There should be a
flexing in the jaw in the turning direction, rather than a
bend in shoulder and neck. This elaborate procedure may
seem more complicated than necessary, but in equitation
seemingly unimportant details can not be overlooked
without disastrous consequences. In this case, the purpose
is to retain control of the horse, both front and rear.

BACKING

Making the horse step backwards is another movement that looks so simple on the surface. It seems that anybody should be able to do it the first time in the saddle. Just pull on the reins. If not immediately successful, pull harder. The trouble is that a good horseman wants it done smoothly and easily, without use of force. To make this possible, the horse must be flexed, light in the hand, and chewing on the bit. In other words, he must be properly balanced so that he will lift his feet and step backwards without leaving the furrows on the ground, indicating that he had dragged his feet, a sure sign of strong-arm technique.

The correct procedure is to assume a light seat by pulling the small of the back in, not by leaning forward; it is accompanied by lively taps with the boots and short, light, increasingly insistent pulls on the reins.

STARTING THE CANTER

The use of the aids in starting the canter is complicated by the fact that the "lead" is involved. The popular method of suddenly leaning forward and kicking the horse violently in the ribs may be necessary for a green student to get results, but the horse's action when cantering and the lead should be explained right from the beginning, in order to create a clear image in the pupil's mind of how he is balanced and how he moves his legs in this gait.

Running loose in the pasture, a horse will automatically take left lead turning to the left and right lead turning right. He just obeys a natural sense of balance. In the school ring the student learns how to control the lead both in a turn and on the straight-away, from a trot, from a walk, and from the spot. He should eventually be able to get and maintain right lead turning left and vice versa.

There are two schools of thought concerning control of the lead when starting to canter. One side argues that the key to the problem is in the forehand and it depends on which front leg reaches out first, ahead of the other. The opposition maintains that the lead is decided in the hindquarters and that the horse prepares himself for left lead by balancing himself on the left hindleg, which is brought forward into a more supporting position. The left front leg will then automatically step out in left lead.

It seems to me that the solution of the problem is quite simple. It all depends on how experienced the rider is. A beginner who does not know how to collect his horse should use the first mentioned technique and proceed as follows: the horse's head is pulled out toward the wall, which to a certain extent "liberates" his inside shoulder and front leg and encourages this leg to reach forward in the first beat of canter. In this position the horse is animated by lively boot action, while the rider leans slightly forward, just enough to be able to follow his horse smoothly.

This method is far from being reliable, particularly when moving on a straight line. It may result in a "cross canter"—one lead in front and another behind. In equitation this method can only be classified as primitive, an emergency measure to make it possible for a beginner to get acquainted with the canter. Being based on the wrong fundamental principles it will lead nowhere if the student is interested in anything but the most superficial forms of equitation and is satisfied with using the noblest animal in existence just for transportation or phony strutting in a show ring.

5. System in Schooling

Learning to ride should be a systematic building process, not an accumulation of scattered, disconnected details. It is also important that the instructor carefully explains the practical reason for everything. A qualified instructor will do this and encourage questions and discussions. Phony explanations are frequently more harmful than no explanations at all. It is not necessary to be a halfwit to become a good horseman, although it may be helpful if the object is rough-riding.

I also believe that youngsters should learn the true facts about horses, their mental and physical abilities, and limitations. I fail to see how the following "true story" in a newspaper recently can add to a child's understanding. It seemed that a little girl fell into a well and was unable to get out. Fortunately, her pet horse was loose in the yard. He heard her yell for help, took hold of the rope attached to a water bucket with his teeth, lowered the bucket into the well, braced his legs and hoisted the little girl, hanging to the bucket. The story was not meant as a joke. But then we hear about horses who can talk, too.

Some people are fortunate enough to be constructed physically to fit the saddle without discomfort. Others need a bit of remodeling before they feel at ease. Adjustment of difficulties of this kind is important and must be given close attention by the instructor.

The following is an example of how a beginners' class should be conducted. More detailed explanation of various movements will be found in succeeding chapters.

BEFORE MOUNTING—Check position of saddle. Make sure that saddle blanket or felt is pulled up from withers, that the girth is properly tightened, that the bit is not

too low or too high in the mouth, that the jaw strap
is not too tight, that the safety locks attaching the
stirrups to the saddle are closed but not stuck. The
student should also be shown how to pick up the
horse's feet to inspect shoes, clean the frog and remove rocks.

MOUNTING—The correct and common-sense way to mount
is important. The most practical way is also the safest.
Teaching to mount also without stirrups, with or
without help, should not be neglected.

MOUNTED—Demonstration of position of seat, legs and
hands with explanation of the reasons for everything.

ELEMENTARY PRACTICE IN USE OF AIDS—From the very beginning the student should acquire the habit of setting
his horse in motion by repeated taps with the boots.
No violent kicks. Also get used to stopping the horse
with several gentle pulls. Under no circumstances
any strong-arm jerks. Stress importance of constant
animation by the boots and the equally constant play
of wrist and fingers on the reins. Later, rhythmical
application of the boots in all gaits replaces the irregular action.

CALISTHENICS IN THE SADDLE (VOLTIGE)—Gymnastic exercises on horseback depend on the gentleness of the
horse. Stirrups must be removed. A blanket instead
of saddle is even better. Reins should be tied in a knot
within easy reach. Mild movements—swinging one
leg at a time with straight knee, bending and turning
torso without displacing seat—can be followed by
swinging one leg at a time over horse's neck, over the
croup, riding backwards, doing the "scissors." Active
youngsters will enjoy these acrobatics also at a trot
and even a canter when jumping off and on again in
one bound becomes possible.

PROGRESSIVE USE OF AIDS—After the limbering-up period
practicing turns and circles should follow. Coordinated use of the aids in changing direction is the

purpose as well as understanding of correct performance.

POSTING—A period of work at a slow trot is followed by a
few turns around the track at an extended trot. Posting is then desirable to avoid interfering with the
horse's free stride. Changing of diagonals. Rhythmic
application of boots.

BACKING—To make the horse step backwards is an excellent
exercise in coordinating the aids. Practice should aim
at fluency in the execution of trot-walk-halt-back-
walk-trot.

SHORT TURN—Pull in to a halt three feet inside the track.
The important part of the movement as a schooling
exercise for both horse and rider is to prevent tendency to back up and to take more than one step
under full control.

CANTER—This should be postponed till satisfactory progress in balance and control makes it safe. Watching
other horses cantering to get understanding of "lead"
is recommended. Begin by starting canter in a corner.
Change lead first by using diagonal of arena, then by
volting with reverse. Changing lead on straight-way
should allow enough intermediate trot to give the
rider time to re-adjust his balance and aids.

FLEXING—Increase emphasis on position of horse's head
and the complete flexing of the jaw, resulting from a
"live" bit. Guard against over-flexing, boring and getting "behind the bit." The horse's straining to "go"
must never be discouraged.

DISMOUNTING—Should be practiced both in the formal manner by swinging the right leg over the croup and,
more informally, by swinging the leg forward, across
the neck, with the hands on the cantle.

This is a standard type of lesson and can be used for
all beginners, with a few modifications for very young
children.

6. Advanced Studies

An obvious proponent of modern conceptions told me not long ago that he was the owner of a fine horse and that he felt the urge to win cups and glory offered by horse shows. But he felt he needed a few pointers regarding jumping. How long would it take to master the technicalities? He admitted that his previous experience consisted of weekend rides, Western style, for which he had not thought it necessary to take any instruction.

I tried to explain why it would be advisable to start from scratch and absorb a few elementary and useful facts in the school ring. His dignity was offended and his suspicions of my mercenary intentions aroused. He tactfully hinted that he was well able to handle any ornery critter without danger of falling off and that he did not have any time to waste on childish stuff.

There are no short cuts in horsemanship, and as far as elementary schooling is concerned, a foundation of common principles is essential, whether the student should later wish to specialize in dressage, jumping, polo, or just plain recreational horseback riding.

There is one fact that soon becomes obvious to any student who takes his preliminary schooling seriously: life is too short to learn all there is to learn about handling a horse under saddle. There seems to be no end to the possibilities, and each small step of progress creates ever increasing satisfaction and new ambitions.

The following is an attempt to sketch a rough outline of an hour in the school ring for an advanced class. The sequence of exercises is about the same as already described for beginners. The difference is that the building

A well-collected horse is necessary in dressage; his endurance and general efficiency are enhanced in every-day riding.

process continues. While the attention in an elementary class centers on the position and actions of the rider, the performance of the horse gradually becomes the sole objective of advanced instructions.

LIMBERING UP—After careful checking and adjustment of saddle and bridle before mounting, the horse is walked around the ring alternately on both hands. An active, full stride is required with the reins loose.

COLLECTION STARTED—The reins are gathered up while animation is increased, resulting in shorter steps, complete flexing, and distinct changes of balance from forehand to hindquarters.

VOLTES—The diameter of the volte depends on the rider's ability to "ride it out," completely round without losing or disturbing the even bend of the horse's body. As experience and training progresses, the diameter should be gradually decreased and become more effective as a collecting movement. In a small volte the horse may be balanced so strongly over his inside hindleg that he will show signs of lifting his forehand into a canter.

EXTENDED TROT—Short periods of collecting movements should be followed by a turn or two around the track at a free trot, taking advantage of the increased collection to lengthen the stride without increasing the beat.

THE SHORT TURN—For the beginner this simple movement provides practice in coordinating the use of the aids. A more advanced rider is expected to demonstrate complete control. The short turn is not a collected movement. The horse should remain flexed and attentive, well on the bit, with no tendency to back. A distinct stop between each step is required.

PARADES—A half parade means pulling the horse in from a faster to a slower gait. A full parade means a full stop. Correct execution should give the impression of balance and ease. Both during and after the parade the horse must remain light in the hand and stop with his hindlegs well under. Starting to advance after a full parade he should begin by moving a front leg instead of having to pull his hindlegs under before he can get going. He should in fact be so well collected that he is ready to lift his forehand into a canter or back without dragging his feet. A parade is a collecting exercise as well as another practice in coordination. The pull on the reins in a parade, transmitted through the seat, is aimed at the hindlegs. In order to insure this, the horse's head should be in a somewhat lowered position and the contact with the horse's mouth below the level of the rider's hands.

BACKING—As usual in more advanced equitation, the horse's form and balance is the essential feature to be watched in stepping backwards. If he is not perfectly collected and a stiff jaw and neck makes a hard pull on the reins necessary, the result will be clumsily dragging feet. A fluent combination of a full parade, immediately followed by a few steps back and advance, without break of motion is recommended.

ADVANCING—After proper preparations the horse should give the impression of alert eagerness and controlled impatience to go into action. This does not mean that he should step around excitedly like a race horse at the gate. He demonstrates his discipline by remaining immovable, until a slight loosening on the reins indicates permission to advance. If he has been collected the way he should, he will then start with a front leg. The most serious offense that can be made during this operation is to be caught in such a position that he has to drag his hindlegs under him before he can get going. As the degree of training, both of horse and rider, improves, the horse, standing at attention, should be able to start both walk, trot and canter from the spot without fumbling.

THE TWO-TRACK—The elementary principle of the two-track is to walk or trot the horse in a slightly sideways position, with the hindquarters following a track to the left or the right of the track of the forehand. With the horse's body straight from nose to tail the two-track is not a collected or collecting movement. But if the oblique position is combined with a sideways flexing of the jaw, a bending of neck and body, a hindleg will be forced into a more supporting position and an important feature has been created of the horse's schooling in advanced equitation.

Let us suppose that a two-track has been started, riding left hand, by wheeling the forehand inside the track. A more pronounced flexing to the left together with increased action of the right boot, well back, will produce a slight bend in the entire body and bring the left hindleg forward. If the horse is moving with his hindquarters inside the track and is again flexed and bent to the left, the effect on the left hindleg will be the same. Obviously the same results can be obtained without changing hands, as far as the right hindleg is concerned, by bending the horse in the opposite direction, with his hindquarters inside and outside the track respectively.

THE PIROUETTE—Everybody who has watched a Western Horse Opera will be familiar with the Hollywood technique of making an abrupt turn: The rider starts the turn ahead of his bronc with a twist of his body, his rein hand come up and yanks violently sideways, the horse's head flies up higher than the rider's and somehow he succeeds in scrambling around in a panic with his legs all tangled up.

This performance has, of course, nothing to do with civilized horsemanship, even of the more primitive kind. It can only be classified as aggravated abuse. A look inside a horse's mouth will make this obvious. The bit normally rests directly on the bare gums of the lower jaw. These gums are no less sensitive than your own, and the bit in this case was originally constructed for the sole purpose of inflicting pain. Today, four hundred years after its conception, it still has the same effect, even though it cannot break the jaw in two, since the chain is no longer permitted.

As an instrument of guidance it is worse than useless. The wild tossing of the horse's head that you
admire so much on the screen is his desperate attempt
to save himself from the pain inflicted by the violent
manipulation of a medieval instrument of torture.

A pirouette consists of spinning the horse around
with the hindquarters as a hub. This is an important
movement and every horseback rider should know
how to do it. A dude's technique may not be spectacular enough to suit the producers of Westerns, but
it has the advantage of being both practical and
effective. Besides, it doesn't hurt the horse at all; in
fact, he usually seems to accept it as a pleasant
game as soon as he catches on to it.

Let us assume that a small circle, correctly executed, is gradually made smaller and smaller, with
the hindquarters kept firmly in by the outside boot
and moving on a smaller circle than the track of the
forehand. As the radius of these practice turns is
decreasing, a moment will arrive when the hindlegs
come to a complete stop while the front legs continue
their circling. A small half volte has been turned
into a pirouette.

The action of the aids during this movement is, as
usual, logical and easily understood by any properly
trained horse. In a pirouette to the left, for instance,
the rider's weight, transferred strongly to the left
seat knuckle, helps to anchor the left hindleg and
keep it stationary. The action of the right boot, applied well back, prevents the hindquarters from slipping out; the vigorous use of the right rein, pushing
against the shoulder, will keep the forehand turning.
The left boot provides the necessary animation. It
also has the important duty to prevent backing.

Effortless and smooth fluency is always a sign of
good riding. You do not have to be an expert to

appreciate this part of it. The execution of a pirouette
is no exception. This means that there are no stops
or breaks in the rhythm. If the pirouette is executed
from a walk, the front legs maintain their regular
beat. If it is done from a trot or a canter, the same
rule applies. A pirouette from a canter is the most
difficult and requires the highest degree of collection,
partly because a change of lead is required.

THE CANTER—A simplified and highly irregular way of ob-
taining the correct lead has already been mentioned
as an emergency measure permitted green beginners.
To the advanced student this seemingly simple operation becomes a more complicated problem. It is no
longer enough to persuade the horse somehow to
start cantering, taking advantage of the most favorable conditions, corners for instance, to take the
correct lead. The able horseman wants to know how
to start the canter with the desired lead on a straight
line, right from the spot, from a walk or a trot. He
wants to have complete control of the lead so that
he can change it at will and with the least possible
delay. To him the important problem is the lead.
He should, for instance, be able to get right lead
during a turn to the left.

Careful study of the horse while he is preparing
himself for the canter will clearly establish the fact
that the lead is decided in the hindquarters, not by
the forehand. A slow-motion movie will show that
he starts by gathering his hindlegs under himself in
a more supporting position. Then, if he seems to be
leaning slightly to the left, with the left hindleg in
front of the right, he is all set to lift his forehand
into a canter in left lead.

Keeping this image in mind, the rider's efforts
should be aimed at assisting the horse in doing what
his instinctive feel of balance tells him to do; it makes

no difference whether the canter is started from the spot, from a walk or a trot, in a turn or on a straight line.

The first move is to animate the horse by increasingly active boots accompanied by a driving seat, while he is checked with both reins. This will get the hindlegs into a more supporting position, providing a complete flexing of the neck is maintained. The next step is to exert the heaviest possible pressure on the left side of the saddle, if left lead is the objective. The action of the right boot is then applied a trifle further back than the left. The left boot animates, the right prevents the hindquarters from swinging out.

During these preparations neck and head should be pointed straight forward, although a very slight, barely noticeable flexing in the jaw to the left may be permitted in order to make quite sure that there is no stiffness or resistance in the left side to oppose the free forward motion of the left shoulder.

There is a muscle running along the crest of a horse's neck from the withers to the ears. It is a reliable sign that he really is flexed to the left, for instance, when his neck is arched and you see this muscle slipping over to the left.

Unless the horse is untrained and unable to understand and react to the aids, he should start the canter by lifting his forehand and retain his collected form. Any tendency to throw himself forward in a rush and "run away from his hindlegs" must be prevented. In more advanced training he should remain so well in hand and balanced in collected canter that a pirouette can be executed at any time. If the canter is started from a walk or a trot, there should, in fact, be a distinct slowing down of the tempo at the start of the canter.

To control the horse at a canter the rider must possess suppleness and ability to follow the movements of his horse smoothly. He must also have a well-developed feel of how to distribute and effectively use his weight in the right place and in the right manner. This is the key to any horse's performance in this gait and also the ultimate test of a horseman.

Although passive relaxation will allow the rider to follow the movements of his horse smoothly, it reduces the effectiveness of his weight and seat as an aid. The active, driving impulses through the seat are necessary to preserve the collected form and are also important in connection with balancing. The horse will pay attention to a seat knuckle digging down, but he may ignore the pressure of a dead weight. The rider's back and loin muscles can never be allowed to remain slack and inactive in the collected gaits. In order to assure the effectiveness of the most important means of communication between rider and horse, they must be in constant action, guided by feel rather than mechanical technique.

Generally speaking, the rider's position in collected work is as it should be when he is pressing down as hard as possible on his seat. The forward urging push is synchronized with the rhythmic taps by the boots at the moment when the hindlegs are in motion forward, creating a muscle reflex that will carry them an inch or two farther.

As previously explained, the importance of a gently playing bit that keeps jaw and neck flexed can not be over-emphasized. The checking with the reins, which at a collected canter meets and absorbs the animating action of seat and boots, is also more effective when used in step with the horse; it is applied when the forehand is off the ground.

In collected movements the horse must never be allowed to lean on the bit.

EXTENDED CANTER—At an extended canter (not gallop) there are other problems to be taken into consideration. The horse must be allowed to transfer more of his weight forward. He will carry his head somewhat lower with a corresponding stretching of the neck. But he is still required to be light in the hand and balanced so that he can easily and quickly be turned, pulled in, or let out at a full gallop. In order to avoid hampering the free action of back and hindquarters, the rider will ease the pressure of the seat, not by standing in the stirrups, but by stronger support in the crotch and on the thighs. Boot action will remain active and the bit supporting.

Both when discussing the lead in connection with the start of the canter and the change of lead in more advanced schooling, it is necessary to have a clear picture of the horse's action in this gait. It seems to me that the key to the problem is the fact that a hindleg is the first to move, making the first beat, followed by the other hindleg and the diagonally opposite frontleg which move simultaneously. The second front leg comes last. Canter has three beats, not four.

A student of elementary horsemanship can not be expected to have much control of his horse's hindlegs and should be allowed to start cantering where it is natural to the horse to take the correct lead— during as sharp a turn as is possible in a corner. An advanced student, however, must aim at full control of the lead.

For practical purposes changing lead may not be of vital importance even to a polo player who has other things on his mind than the "coordinated use of the aids." At an extended canter the horse will take care of such little details by himself, but it will make it much easier for him if timely transfer of the rider's weight gives him timely warning and help.

For schooling purposes, however, both as far as horse and rider are concerned, control of the lead is important and interesting as part of the art of equitation. Every moment of progress—starting with change of hand and lead by riding diagonals through the arena, figure eights in the big volte, small voltes with reverse, change on the straight-away with two or three beats of trot in between, keeping right lead turning sharply left—towards the goal (changing lead every stride) has more fascination to the serious student than any other part of his curriculum.

GALLOP—This gait belongs exclusively on the race track, but is unfortunately also popular with a certain breed of bridle trail jockeys.

All I have to say about it is: DON'T DO IT.

POSTING—Some of my cowboy friends of long ago down in Texas doubled up with merriment and yowled like hungry hyenas the first time they caught me posting. Soon everybody was posting and hee-hawing all over the place. I was the only one riding Western style. A reaction like this might have been encouraging, if I had been there as a missionary preaching the gospel of International Technique. But I was only a visitor, hoping to pick up some information regarding the activities of the North American Cowboy and the reason why he has acquired so much fame and admiration. I must confess, however, that after looking at the posting business through the eyes of the cow pokes for a few weeks, I found myself sharing their opinion. It looked kind of comical, and I have still not been able to entirely get rid of that impression, in spite of the fact that posting can be a graceful movement if it is done correctly.

Not so very long ago, education at riding academies was regarded as finished as soon as the student was able to post after a fashion. The advantage was obvious even to the greenest beginner. It was so much more pleasant than being shaken silly by the rough bumps when sitting down on the trot. It also was a time- and money-saving device, because you avoided the tedious and painful process of acquiring the suppleness and balance that seemed hopeless anyway.

It is still true that posting saves any rider—beginner or veteran—a great deal of punishment, although this is the least important part of its advantages. Since the rider's seat touches the saddle only every other beat of the trot, the horse avoids lugging a more or less dead weight. The rider's weight does not descend in a heavy crash but in a light, brief contact and under full control. The horse soon gets the knack of assisting the rider to rise. This means more vigorous action of back muscles and hindquarters, which again results in increased economy of effort. The importance of all this on long rides is easily understood.

To post, the rider's weight is transferred slightly from the seat to stirrups and knees. The knees are the hinges around which everything moves and they must not be allowed to move or slip. The seat should swing forward as it moves up, the crotch following the incline of the pommel. This will stabilize the balance and give the impression of ease and grace. In other words, during the short moment when the seat touches the saddle, the rider is leaning a trifle forward, a definite straightening up accompanies the lift. The seat should descend into the saddle gently and under full control and touch with its full weight, but with no trace of bumping. A slight stiffening of the back at this moment will facilitate the upward motion and prevent a break in its smooth continuity. By standing in the stirrups and trying to lift himself, the rider will only succeed in looking ridiculous.

In a clean, natural trot the horse moves his legs diagonally, for example, left front leg and right hind-leg simultaneously. If the seat descends at the same time as the left front foot hits the ground, you are posting in the left diagonal. Close attention to this is important. The rider should at all times be aware of which diagonal he is posting on and change for each period of trot. There has been some question about the diagonal to be used in a turn. It has been my experience that coming down on the outside frontleg is both practical and logical. In a sharp turn the horse is leaning to the side he is turning, resulting in a shorter step closer to the ground, while the outside leg swings freely in an extended step. Posting on the inside diagonal seems to be unnatural and liable to encourage stumbling. For the same reason it makes sense to come down on the lower side if the road or path is slanting.

Lack of attention to alternating diagonals may result in stiffness in a horse's side, including the neck, which may lead to several kinds of trouble. He may, for instance, develop a preference for one lead at a canter.

7. The Right Thing at the Right Time

An hour's work in the ring should be carefully planned. It is important that the various movements follow each other in logical sequence. When the horse comes out of the stable in the morning, he needs a period of limbering up and relaxation. He may come out snorting and with his back up and must be allowed to work his exuberance off without too much restraint. It is a serious mistake to subdue his "joie de vivre" by force. He may also be stiff and sore as a result of hard work the previous day and even show a tendency to buck, particularly if the girth has been tightened too hard or too roughly. In either case, the horse must never be ridden actively until he is completely relaxed. Even then he should not be put through any movement that requires collection until he has been walked and trotted for five or ten minutes with a light rein.

The degree of control is increased gradually as the horse willingly accepts the aids. A heavier, driving seat takes the place of the posting, used during the limbering-up period, the animation of the boots becomes more insistent, and the effect is met and gathered up in the hands with special attention to the flexing. The horse is now ready for the standard schooling movements. Turns and small voltes at a walk and trot are alternated by half and full parades, backing and two-track. It is important that these movements are constantly varied and that the ones requiring a maximum of collection, like pirouettes, follow less exacting small voltes and two-track.

The key to successful training of a horse as well as of the rider is *patience*. Successful execution of the schooling movements must not be expected too quickly and must under no circumstances be enforced. They can be per-

78

fected only by endless repetition, often without noticeable improvement from day to day. The rider's natural urge and eager repetition of every movement, impatiently striving to get tangible results quickly, is also a mistake. This is a medicine that should be given in small doses and with judicious intervals.

The periods of collected work should also be strictly limited and frequently interrupted by moderately extended trot with improved action resulting from the collecting exercises. Frequent relaxed walk with long reins, but maintaining a full stride, must not be omitted.

The last 15 or 20 minutes are devoted to work at a canter. As soon as the right tempo has been established, preferably on the "big volte," the horse is put out on the square repeating the routine of small voltes, turns and parades. Two-track is not a canter movement, but the change of lead becomes a new and complicated problem that requires much care and patience. Both instructor and rider should have a clear understanding of the fundamental fact that changing of lead, even in stride or from the spot, comes naturally to the horse. It is not an artificial circus movement. With this important truth as a basis, horse and rider are guided step by step (from first learning) not to interfere with the horse's natural inclination, to helping, controlling and developing his inborn ability.

Progressing from cantering on the track, turning in on the diagonal of the arena, pulling in to a trot towards the center and starting the canter again in the corner with the new lead and aiming at the change of lead in stride on the straight-away, the student will make use of half figure eights in the "big volte," turns with change of hand and small voltes with reverse. The collected movements are interrupted by short periods of extended canter on the track with change of lead, using the diagonal. To dismount and lead the horse at the end of the hour, after loosening the girth, till his respiration is normal, should be a matter of routine.

8. Dressage Is Not Fancy

An equitation class is supposed to demonstrate the rider's ability; a dressage performance concentrates on the schooling of the horse. It is difficult to understand why there can be any difference between the two. Where does equitation end and dressage begin? Both horse and rider are inseparably involved in either case. It is a partnership in which they must share the honor or the blame, regardless of what the exhibition is called. For that matter, where is the dividing line between advanced horsemanship and dressage? It is quite true that a dressage performance is judged by the execution of a few spectacular movements that may have impressed you if you have watched the Lipizzaners in action or the Schuman family riding in their circus.

But the fact of the matter is that the fancy-looking capers of these horses are not tricks performed on certain signals. They are the results of systematic training and developing natural qualities and abilities. Most dressage movements and their background of sound training are of fundamental importance to every horseman, on the trail, in the jumping arena, across open country, on the polo field, or in the show ring. Unfortunately there is a joker in the deck, The rider must be well educated, too.

Here and there, hunter trials and similar events under different names have appeared for the purpose of promoting good horsemanship as well as good horses. The fundamental idea and actually the most important part of the trials is a test in practical dressage, including equitation. The general principles of the three-day event of the Olympic Games apply, but on a more modest level.

The horse is first shown in a training test, which is only a less ambitious name for a dressage exhibition. The same horse and rider next negotiate a cross-country course with a variety of obstacles and finally pass a jumping test in an enclosed arena.

These three tests are by no means independent of each other. They are meant to give a fairly complete picture of the skill and efficiency both of horse and rider, and the training test is by far the most important and revealing, particularly as far as the rider is concerned. It is not an uncommon sight at horse shows to see a good horse drag a poor rider over a few jumps or a rider clinging precariously to the saddle in a cross-country. The practical dressage test will never fail to separate the sheep from the goats. Even if the rider's ability as an equestrian is not on trial, his control of the horse, the horse's response to the aids, his alert obedience, suppleness, efficiency and economy of action will soon reveal what kind of a horseman he is. These elements will determine his success or failure, not only in the training test, but in the cross-country and the jumping as well. No horse is good enough to disguise or completely cover up his rider's shortcomings.

The elementary, practical dressage in which we are interested means development of obedience, alert attention, sensitive response to the aids, improvement of the three natural gaits. These are the necessary requirements that make the "fancy" movements possible.

The least that can be expected of a good horse is that he can be turned, even "spun" around, stand still when required, change gait and tempo, and generally remain under control, regardless of circumstances and without use of brute force. Some kind of training is necessary to do these simple things even in a primitive manner. It makes a lot of difference if they are done well. A little elementary dressage will accomplish this and make work easier both for horse and rider.

There are other advantages, too. A striking development of the muscles will soon become obvious, with corresponding improvement of suppleness and strength. Conformation and appearance in general will change for the better, giving an impression of poise and balance. Vigorous action in the hocks, increased power of the croup, strength of back and shoulders—these are all conspicuous results of the gymnastic exercises provided by practical dressage.

The dressage training begins as soon as the rider has learned to coordinate and use his aids effectively and when the horse at the same time has advanced enough to understand and respond to the aids. The knowledge and practice of elementary dressage methods is the only way for a horseman and his mount to enjoy in full measure the pleasures of riding, which recently appearing "horse trainers" seem well on their way to destroy.

9. A Closer Look

Anybody who has watched horses in action will have noticed that they can not perform efficiently unless their hindlegs are in the right position. It would seem unnecessary to spend time and effort teaching a horse what comes naturally to him. He will start a canter or a gallop by gathering his hindlegs under him. He can not get over a hurdle without doing the same thing. A polo pony or a cutting horse can not twist and turn quickly unless he sits down on his hocks.

All this is obvious enough, but there are, nevertheless, several good reasons why the rider should know how to preserve and improve this inborn ability. Besides, there are circumstances when a horse will not balance and collect himself properly without considerable persuasion. In the slow gaits, for instance, it is natural for him to use the hindlegs for pushing rather than carrying, leaning on his forehand. Standing still, walking or trotting he will lean heavier on his forehand than on his hindquarters, unless he is prevented by the rider. Balanced this way the horse is actually out of hand. He is not prepared to execute a pirouette, he is not ready to start a canter without rushing. Attempts to slow down the tempo at a trot or canter will result in falling into a walk.

While there is no point in collecting an ordinary sport or pleasure horse, until he can perform "courbettes" and "caprioles," the "piaffe" is a realistic goal to aim at. He is then trotting without advancing, with the hocks well under, powerful action in the back, hardly touching the ground with his front feet. The training process to improve the horse's form and balance is the most fascinating

83

part of equitation and can become so absorbing that the collecting exercises are overdone and may result in a horse that is permanently "behind the bit." The dressage enthusiast must under no circumstances lose sight of the fact that if the horse loses his "élan," he is no longer much good for ordinary use. A well-schooled and well-ridden horse is equally ready, at a moment's notice, to stretch out at a full gallop or spin around on his hocks.

BUILDING MUSCLES

Some horses give the impression of being sway-backed. The back seems to be abnormally long and there is a distinct "step" where the spine joins the croup. Horses are, of course, not shaped in the same mold at birth and conformations vary. But there is no mistaking an animal that has been trained along the principles of practical dressage, regardless of his native shape and form. Even if he has been born with a long back, this no longer appears as a noticeable feature. Due to the gymnastics connected with the right kind of training, his back is filled with well-developed muscles, there is no "step" in front of his croup and the well-rounded shape of his hindquarters is not the result of abundant feeding, but of bulging, powerful muscles. His upper arms and shoulders look filled out, too, for the same reason. His physical well being and sense of power is reflected in the way he stands. His head is up, ears pointed forward, eyes alert. He looks like he is raring to go, with all four legs planted solidly under him. He is an athlete and he looks it. No horse, regardless of breed, can give the same impression of quality if his schooling has been of the wrong kind or neglected.

Beauty and harmony of action in all gaits always indicates dressage training. He touches the ground so lightly with his feet that on a hard surface he sounds dramatically different from less fortunate drudges. In well-collected form he can be trotted on hard roads without damage to his feet, because he actually hits the pavement with less force than an unbalanced horse, who comes down more heavily each step on his straight and stiff front legs. Another advantage of being able to control the horse's balance and degree of collection is that the beat at a trot can to a certain extent be regulated. Slowing it down, for instance, under certain circumstances, may contribute to reduce effort and preserve endurance. At a slow, collected trot, this gain can also be maintained riding down long, easy slopes that otherwise would have had to be negotiated at a walk to avoid damage to front legs and shoulders.

MORE ON VOLTES

Returning to the school movements previously discussed—voltes, parades, backing, etc.—it becomes obvious that they have a multiple purpose. The small volte is an example. It will be remembered that the horse in this case is bent from nose to tail. How pronounced the bend is depends on the radius of the volte, which again is decided by the rider's ability as well as the horse's responsiveness. Riding a small volte has no schooling value if the hindquarters are permitted to swing out or the tempo is slowed to a shuffle.

If correctly executed, the repeated practice of the small volte will gradually force one hindleg at a time into a more supporting position and teach the horse to balance himself in this manner by responding to the rider's aids. One proof of the effectiveness of this exercise is that sooner or later it will result in an unexpected lift of the forehand to start a canter. The alternate bending and stretching of the horse's body has the same effect on him as a man's exercises in a gymnasium. It will strengthen the muscle systems of the back, the croup, and the flanks and at the same time develop the suppleness that is equally important.

In addition to all this, the small volte is an important means to school the horse in sensitive response to seat, boots, and reins, which the rider on his part must learn to use with a delicate feel and touch that the horse can understand and trust. The small volte serves its purpose best if it is ridden only once around and followed by another only after a straightening out on the track.

A more advanced use of the volte is in connection with starting the canter and changing of lead. After completing the circle correctly, the horse is balanced perfectly for cantering with the proper lead at the moment when he reaches the track. If the circle is executed at a canter, change of lead can be done by leaving the circle at a tangent, reversing the aids, and resuming the canter in the opposite direction after checking to a few beats of trot, if necessary, on the tangent.

By gradually decreasing the radius of the small volte, a moment will come when the hindlegs stop moving while the front legs pivot around them in a half circle. This is the pirouette. The pirouette is a finished dressage movement and, strictly speaking, not a schooling exercise. Both the student and his horse must be highly experienced before it is attempted. The full weight must be transferred to the hindquarters and although the frontfeet are not required to leave the ground completely, there can be no question of maintaining a beat of any kind. Executed from a canter, change of lead is easily combined with a pirouette by the experienced horseman.

Like all other exercises to improve a horse's balance— to collect him—the parades must be exactly right. Otherwise they are not only useless, but may quite often be harmful. The popular conception is only natural: You slow a horse down or stop him by pulling on the reins. If he won't do so more or less willingly, you use a bit that will hurt him badly if he does not obey. The way it should be done, both for humane and practical reasons, is quite different. It makes it easier for the rider and less painful for the horse if he can be checked quickly and smoothly, even from a full gallop, without the use of brutality and instruments of torture.

MORE ON PARADES

A fundamental requirement is that the horse always be well balanced, flexed, and light in the hand. To train and school him along these lines, practicing correct parades plays an important part. If during this process neck and jaw are well flexed, light pulls on the reins will be enough to check him while seat and boots actively urge him forward. The principle is to stop the forehand a fraction of a second before the hindquarters, with the result that the hindlegs are well under when the parade is over. In this way the checking is performed with ease and the horse is balanced and poised for equally smooth execution of succeeding maneuvers.

In other words, practicing of parades has the same constructive purpose and effect on both horse and rider as the small volte.

MORE ON CANTER

Of all the exercises used in training to develop collection, muscles, suppleness, obedience and, above all, the action in all three gaits, the work at canter is probably the most valuable. This refers particularly to the preparations for canter and the delicate operation of changing lead. This presents problems that a well-educated and ambitious horseman can build up to "High School" movements, but for practical purposes means increased pleasure and efficiency, even if they are not developed much beyond the elementary stage.

BIG VOLTE

The work begins on the "big volte." The advantage
of a curved track is that the rider's aids are then already
in the approximate position to prepare for the canter and
the horse is also more favorably balanced than on a
straight line.

As previously explained, the "big volte" is a circle that
completely fills one end of the rectangular arena. Three-
fourths of it is accordingly supported by the walls or fence.
This is called the "closed" part of the volte. The remaining
fourth, which forms a curve across the arena from one
long side to the other, is the "open" part. The two ends
of this curve, where the volte joins the main track, are
the "parade points."

The horse is taken in on the big volte at the slowest
possible collected trot without losing the active swing of
his back. As soon as he is well balanced and relaxed without being sluggish and the tempo has acquired a machine-
like regularity, the preparations for canter can begin.

Upon leaving the closed part of the volte at one of the
parade points the rider transfers his weight noticeably to
the side he is turning. As usual, it is important that this
transfer consists of increased pressure on the seat knuckle
on that side, produced by sliding the seat over a fraction
of an inch. Bending sideways is not effective.

The animating action of the boot on the same side
simultaneously becomes more pronounced. The neck, particularly close to the shoulders, remains straight, while
the flexing of the jaw already should be assured.

With the increased action of the inside boot, a slight
checking by the outside rein is necessary to prevent any
increase of tempo. The desired response is to make the
horse's hindquarters swing very slightly out, but must
under no circumstances develop into a two-track. All we
want is to be sure that he obeys and responds to seat and
boot, resulting in the inside hindleg stepping a trifle across

and in front of the outside.

This movement is limited to a few beats on the open part of the volte. Approaching the other parade point, the horse is straightened out by application of the outside boot well back. He is then ridden in normal form around the closed part without loss of collection. Reaching the open part again, the operation is repeated.

As soon as the horse responds willingly to seat and inside boot, the outside boot commences counter action, forcing the hindquarters somewhat in and the inside hindleg consequently into a more supporting position. The inside boot gradually becomes more insistent, while the hindquarters no longer are permitted to get outside the track. The rider will notice a trace of limping motion as the horse collects himself more and more over the inside hindleg.

At this stage of the training the rider should not attempt to decide the moment for starting the canter. The horse will start when it becomes the natural thing for him to do so. The canter should at first be retained only half way around the volte, while tempo and collection are carefully preserved. Change of gait to trot is executed by checking with the outside rein. The horse must never be allowed to fall into a trot of his own accord.

It is always noticeable that the first two or three beats of trot after the canter are "rough." The reason for the more vigorous action of the back at this time is that the horse was more collected during the canter and that the effect can be felt, for a short time to begin with, in the succeeding trot. The objective then becomes to maintain the collected form with its strong lifting action of the back for longer and longer periods of trot. The practice of the canter will in this manner be a valuable help to improve the action, not only at a collected trot, but at an extended trot also. In fact, the improvement of the extended trot should become the most spectacular result of collecting dressage.

The work on the big volte should frequently be interrupted by a trip around the main track. This is a waste of time if the purpose is not clearly understood. The objective is to lengthen the steps without increasing the beat. This can be done only if the horse can be kept balanced with his hindlegs well under. If he is allowed to "run away from his hindlegs," he immediately loses the springy action that starts in the hocks and sometimes results in a snap and forward reach of the frontlegs, which is one of the most conspicuously beautiful movements a horse can perform. It looks unhurried and gives the rider the most exhilarating feeling he will ever have in the saddle.

During the work on the big volte, the practice of extended gaits on the main track should be limited to once around occasionally. A stretching of the steps should be attempted only for a few beats on the two long sides. The tempo should be slowed down sharply and the horse collected in each corner.

It usually does not take very long before a decidedly pleasant change can be detected both in action, response, and general behavior. The horse maintains his balance for longer periods at a trot and at a canter. The action of hocks and back become more vigorous and at the same time more pleasant and springy. His tempo at a canter can be slowed without danger of falling apart into a trot. He seems to become lighter in the hand. He seems to be getting more spirited every day, but at the same time more gentle. It is a real pity that the rank and file of horseback riders will never even suspect what they are missing.

How far you can go even in the elementary stages of dressage depends in the first place on how much time and effort you are prepared to allow as well as on other qualifications that you may or may not have. Patience and understanding of a horse's physical and mental limitations are fundamental requirements. Today's improved breeds of horses are with few exceptions qualified for advanced dressage training. If they sometimes seem stubborn, clumsy and unwilling, it is safe to guess that the original trainer is to blame. It is also safe to say that incompetent trainers are doing more harm both to young and older horses than the best of horsemen can repair.

It is difficult to say who benefits the most by the sometimes tedious but always absorbing process of teaching a horse to change lead at a canter. A rough-rider does not, of course, give any thought to such fancy stunts. It is up to the horse to see to it that he does not fall over his own feet! But again, the rider is the loser. He is missing a fascinating and rewarding part of equitation that can develop his abilities as a horseman. A high degree of control is required to change lead even with several beats of trot in between to give him time to readjust his aids, building up to the ultimate goal of changing the lead in stride or having the lead decided when starting the canter from the spot.

The work is most conveniently begun on the big volte by riding half a figure eight from one parade point to the other. Just before reaching the center the horse is pulled in to a trot. In passing the center the rider quickly shifts his aids to balance him for the new lead. The horse will soon begin to understand what it is all about, and from then on progress will depend on how quickly and effectively the rider himself can make his readjustments. As performance improves, a full figure eight can also be used. Always keep in mind not to overdo highly collected and demanding exercises of this kind without frequent limbering on the main track.

Variations, like using small voltes with reverse, can also be recommended to avoid the lethargy that goes with monotony. You can also practice on the straight-away and retain a controlled false lead in a turn.

As previously mentioned, the objective is the changing of the lead in stride. Although the ponies are doing it all

the time on the polo field to save their balance, it is a
High School movement, and for the average student it is
the training practice that is of value. Nevertheless, it is
useful to have an idea of how a "changement à tempo"
is performed. There is an incorrect way that is easily mistaken for the real thing. This is done "on the ground." If
the horse, for instance, is cantering in left lead and it is remembered how his legs are moving (left hindleg, left
frontleg and right hindleg simultaneously, left frontleg),
he can change lead with his left front foot on the ground.
This is the easiest way, but it is not accepted as correct.
It should be done at the moment when both front feet are
off the ground. That is when the right hindleg is moving
forward into position for right lead.

10. How to Measure Ability

In order to judge a rider's ability it is necessary to obtain a picture of him that will reveal all his virtues as well as all his shortcomings. Present confused ideas about technique make this practically impossible, and the only way out of the dilemma is to limit the test to a primitive simplicity that permits everybody to take part—something like the "Seat and Hands" classes.

The following two series of movements are examples of what comprehensive tests of horsemanship look like. The beginners are judged on their position and their use of the aids with resulting control of their horses. In the advance class these points are secondary to the performance of the horse in movements of elementary dressage.

BEGINNERS

1. Inspection of saddling and bridling
2. Mounting and dismounting
3. Questions regarding horse's anatomy and care, safety rules and etiquette
4. Movements at a walk:
   Full parade
   Small volte
   Back
   Short turn
5. Movements at slow trot:
   Full parade
   Small volte
   Back
6. Movements at extended trot:
   Posting
   Half parade to slow trot
   Big figure eight, change diagonal

93

7. Movements at canter
Start with correct lead in passing corner
Big figure eight with half parade and change of lead
8. Token jump

ADVANCED

1. Inspection of saddling and bridling
2. Mounting
3. Movements at a walk:
Small volte
Full parade
Back
Two-track
Pirouette
4. Movements at collected trot:
Small volte
Full parade
Back
Pirouette
5. Movements at extended trot:
Full parade
Back
Big figure eight, change diagonal
Half parade to collected trot
6. Movements at collected canter:
Small volte
Small volte with reverse and change of lead (not more than three beats of intermediate trot)
Full parade
Start of canter from walk, collected trot, and halt
7. Movements at extended canter:
Big figure eight with half parade to trot and change of lead
8. Three jumps at judge's discretion, no wings
9. Dismounting
10. Questions regarding handling of emergencies

11. Jumping

At the time when I was a cavalry cadet in Norway, part of our equestrian education took place in "Nightmare Alley," freely translated. This consisted of a straight track or lane that was 200 to 300 yards long and about 30 feet wide. Once inside, there was no way to escape except through the exit gate at the other end. The fences on both side were constructed of solid rails and almost as high as a mounted man's head.

Triple bar, bush and rail (Olympic model).

Between the entrance gate and the exit there were a number of obstacles that your horse had to pass, one way or another. He had no choice and was well aware of it. We always thought that these obstacles were the creations of an evil mind and with an abnormal imagination. We never found out to whom it belonged. There were solid log walls, in-and-outs, ditches, bales of hay, a broken-down farm wagon or two, a high bank—all of them arranged in the most unattractive combinations possible.

A man stationed at the exit gate with a bucket full of carrots or oats encouraged the horses to lose no time in reaching the other end. They needed no persuasion and the riders had nothing to worry about except to hang on.

Since no fine points of technique were involved, saddles were regarded as unnecessary, and since the horses needed no guiding, bridles were often discarded, too. The reins were then tied in a knot and left hanging, enabling some of the more dashing recruits to gallop through the course with their arms nonchalantly crossed. Some of us may have fallen off occasionally, but nobody was hurt, as far as I can remember.

Needless to say, this kind of training did wonders both for horses and riders. It gave us a confidence and developed a sense of balance that nothing else could have done. The horses became sure-footed and learned to adjust their stride for take-offs in jumps of all kinds, without the use of whips or other forms of encouragement. Like all other training in European cavalry at the time, it was based on the reward system. Wherever schooling of horses was taking place, there always was a man present with a bucket of oats or other delicacies. It is impossible to obtain even remotely comparable results by the brutal methods of today, which are aimed at destroying the most precious part of a good horse's makeup—his spirit and courage.

The more formal part of our instruction in jumping took

Brush, rail and water jump (Olympic model).

place in the indoor school ring, where the detailed technique of handling the horse before, during and after the jump was thoroughly analyzed using a single, easy barrier, usually a pole heavily padded with straw. We also used outdoor arenas with varied, standard-type jumps, arranged along the same lines as in horse shows, to practice the even, controlled tempo and action that should characterize the performance under such circumstances.

A popular event at our horse shows at that time was a class called "Surprise Obstacles." Nobody knew in advance what they would be like except that there always would be something that no horse had ever been asked to jump before. Among the endless variations I can remember things like a dining table complete with plates and glasses, an ice bucket with a bottle of champagne and several well-dressed dummies made of straw sitting around the table. Another invention was something that looked like a barbed-wire fence but actually was con-

structed of knitting yarn and pine needles. To make it possible for your horse to see it, you had to dismount and hang your coat over it, climb aboard again, jump it practically from the spot, and get off and on again while you retrieved your coat.

At least once there were three big beer barrels, on end,

beside each other, with a closed line of quart bottles (full) on top of them. There were, of course, no wings to any of these jumps. The riders could claim possession of any and all bottles left standing, providing the horse did not balk at the unfamiliar sight. It is understandable why this item reappeared as a "surprise" for several seasons.

Still another thing I can remember, because I had some embarrassing trouble with it myself, was a 12-foot-long metal cylinder. It seemed to be hollow and two or three feet in diameter. Pulled by two men, it rolled slowly up and down the middle of the arena. To make it even more unattractive, it appeared to have some loose rocks inside that made it rattle. We were supposed to jump this thing while it was moving, both coming and going. I have always felt that the most convincing test of a horse's con-

Bank and rails used in Olympic Games.

fidence in his rider and, at the same time, the degree of the rider's control, was the so-called "obedience jumps." They consisted of a regular type fence, without wings, that gradually was made more and more narrow until it was no wider than it was high.

The ability to jump is natural to a horse, and if he has been trained the way he should, he will always regard it as a form of play. I have more than once seen horses running loose in a field, where something to jump was available and deliberately turn aside to sail over it just for fun.

In appearance a good jumper or hunter is rarely glamorous. He is not of the flashy type whose only accomplishment is to strut around a show ring with a broken tail sticking up and capering in a manner that no horse was meant to act.

His beauty lies in the impression he gives, even standing at ease, of power, harmony and poise. His shoulders are sloping, his neck is long and gracefully curved. The withers are high and so long that the back seems abnormally short. The powerful, somewhat sloping croup and the solid padding of muscles of hindquarters and back makes this part of him look like it is taller than the front part. Another significant characteristic is the wide and strongly bent hocks and the relatively short cannons and free tendons. If he has been fortunate enough to avoid mistreatment during the training period, he will receive you with friendly attention when you approach him and he will tackle a jump with an expression of eager courage instead of the terror-distended, white-glinting eyes of the whip-trained animal.

In building up an efficient jumper the development of strong muscles is, of course, important, but at the same time, a systematic encouragement of his "élan" must not be neglected. His natural urge to "go" must at all cost be preserved.

Practice of the previously described collected move-

Ditch and rails, Olympic Games type. The ditch came as a surprise to this horse, but he made it, thanks to rider's unorthodox but effective acrobatics.

ments will have the same effect on a horse's co-ordination and strength as the proper kind of gymnastics has on humans, but the resulting response and obedience are even more important, both in the show ring and in the open country. These exercises should go hand in hand with carefully adjusted jumping practices, which will do more harm than good if they are over-done to such an extent that the horse becomes discouraged. The trainer must always insist on obedience but use extreme care not to demand the impossible and then attempt to overcome justified opposition by using force.

Frequent intervals of extended canter and gallop must not be neglected. Stamina and wind are just as important as muscles, which must be prevented from becoming

A well-trained jumper should take strange and unexpected obstacles in his stride and with confidence. They can never be accomplished by the "whiptraining and poling" technique.

knotted. Horses can become muscle-bound like humans.

One of the most valuable and effective ways to develop the qualities of a jumper is to walk him up and down steep inclines. This also has the advantage of doing no damage even if it is exaggerated.

A training procedure like this requires much time, but no short cuts are possible if the best results are to be expected. It is regretable from every point of view that modern dilettante owners and trainers do not feel that they can afford to spend so much time. They want results quickly, and since few of them qualify for the title of "horseman," they devise ways and means to get the horse ready for the next horse show, mostly by jumping him in-

cessantly, week after week, with generous use of force. Most of these horses are further handicapped by the fact that when they get in the show ring, they will practically be on their own. Chances are that the person in the saddle has had little or no schooling in equitation and can be of no help to his horse. Frequently such riders actually interfere with their mounts and add to their troubles.

To "lift" a horse over a fence is an expression frequently heard among Mutual Admiration Society experts. It has always made me slightly ill for a variety of reasons. Exactly how much a rider can actively influence his horse while negotiating a series of jumps depends in the first place on how well trained the horse is, how well he has learned to adjust his stride for the take-off, his physical condition and his spirit or lack of it. Jumping is also a test of the rider's education and training. Most important is his delicate sense of balance that makes it possible for him to adjust his weight at the right moments, follow his horse smoothly and avoid throwing him off balance. Good hands are just as necessary in jumping as in dressage. Involuntary jerks and pulls on the reins are fully as disturbing as insecure balance.

The fundamental requirement in jumping is, in other words, to remain passive, but it must be an educated passiveness that means complete control of arms and legs and all the rest, including the section above the collar bone. There are, of course, occasions when even the best trained horse needs a little active assistance, and a good rider is expected to be prepared for this at all times.

Efficient performance depends a great deal on the tempo during the approach. It is up to the rider to regulate this with the utmost care and to collect his horse between jumps, keep his hindlegs well under him and his jaw flexed, light in the hand. During the take-off, the flight and the landing he must be allowed full freedom of head and neck, but he should be gathered up again as quickly as possible in preparation for the next jump. The best rate of speed for various types of jumps can not always be left for the horse to decide. Even the best of them need a helping hand and success or failure depends on the rider's ability.

An increase of tempo is called for when approaching a wide ditch, for instance, but the process must be handled with care. If the horse is collected the way he should be before starting the approach, a slight loosening of the reins should be enough. If he is allowed or urged to speed up a trifle too much, he may "run away from his hindlegs" and have to depend on his momentum alone to carry him across; he will not be in a position to execute that last powerful push, which is equally important. To collect the horse for a high jump, all that should be necessary is a judicious checking without change of position, unless he should show signs of balking. In that case the seat must come down, driving hard, accompanied by trip-hammer action of the boots. With resistance overcome, the success of the jump will then depend on the quickness of the rider's change from a heavy to a forward seat, the smooth transfer of his center of gravity to avoid being dragged over by the reins.

When I was a boy, we had a fine English print in color hanging over the sofa. It presented a scene from a fox hunt. In the foreground a great, gray horse had just cleared a fence and in the saddle a well-nourished, red-faced squire was leaning back so far that his shoulders almost touched the horse's rump. His fat legs were sticking straight forward, his left hand clutching the reins, his right waving a hunting crop over his head. I realized already at that time that this was poor form and it led me to suspect that the British had ideas about riding that differed considerably from Continental perceptions. I found out later that the frantic pose of the red-coated squire may have been justified by circumstances, regardless of what the artist's intentions may have been. It is always possible that this particular horse was meant to illustrate the dramatic moment when he was headed for a nose dive after failing to clear the fence. In that case, and similar emergencies, the best of horsemen must be justified in trying to save himself by using informal methods.

The rider's hands during jumping should be given very special attention. They should be safely anchored in such a way that the possibility of disturbing the horse by involuntary jerks on the reins is eliminated. Between jumps the position of the hands must permit free manipulation of the reins to keep them properly adjusted, regulate the tempo and preserve the horse's balance. As soon as the approach begins, the steady support of the reins is important to give him confidence. The hands are then placed firmly on the crest, leaning on the balls of the thumbs with only a light grip on the reins, permitting them to slide out between the fingers when the horse demands more rein. Inexperienced riders, whose balance is still insecure, should be advised to take a solid hold of mane or crest. The hands must at all cost be prevented from leaving their position. If this should happen, the result will not only be a heavy jerk on the reins but loss of balance followed by a heavy bump into the saddle, leading to more trouble.

As previously mentioned, the normal position as well as its variations are decided by the laws of equilibrium, which, to the green horseman is limited to its elementary principle: "What has gone up, has to come down." Unfortunately, it is not that simple, when the inertia of one object, attached to another that is in motion, is involved.

It is common sense that the action of a jumping horse's back and hindquarters should not be hampered. It is further obvious that the rider's center of gravity should be placed where the horse would want it. If you have ever carried a heavy pack on your back, you know what I mean. The rider will accomplish this by leaning forward, taking his weight off his seat and distributing it on thighs, knees and stirrups with his crotch supported against the pommel. His center of gravity should be as close to the horse as possible and his seat consequently lifted just enough to be out of reach of the back action. To depend too much on the support of the stirrups reduces stability.

A well-trained horse is accustomed to the un-interrupted guidance of the aids. It gives him confidence, and if it is interrupted he may become confused. The principle of passivity has been stressed previously but should not be exaggerated to such an extent that the rider loses touch with his horse. For this reason, the horse must be aware of the boots at all times in order to respond quickly when necessary.

Another detail that should not be overlooked is the position of the heel. When spurs are carried, the reason for a low heel is obvious. The low heel also keeps the calf muscle tensed, firm and more effective as an aid, and prevents the lower leg from slipping back too far.

CONVENTIONAL JUMPS

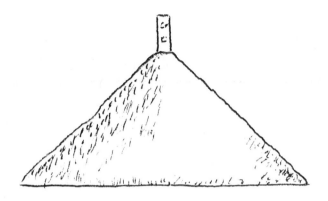

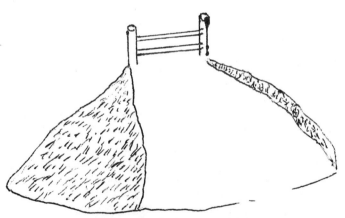

Italian Bank (top: profile).

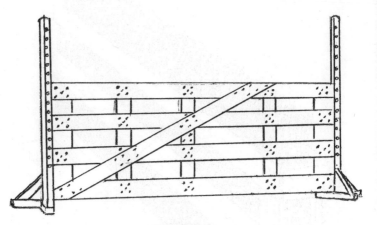

Panel Gate.

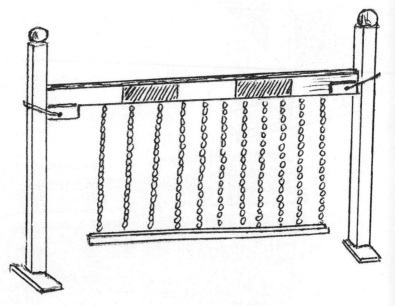

Continental Railroad Gate.

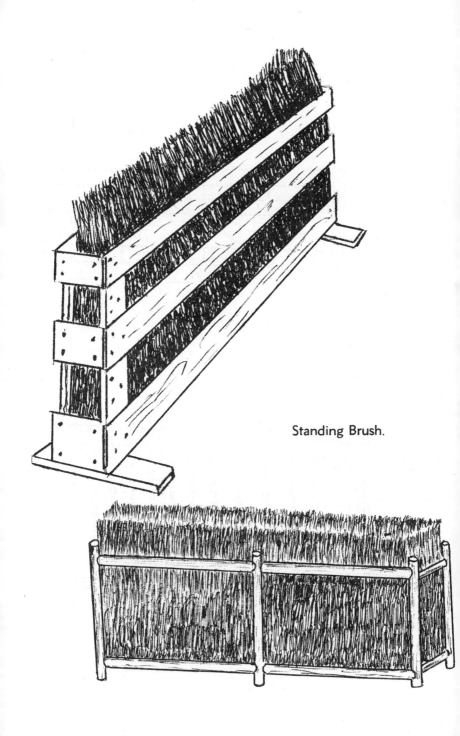

Standing Brush.

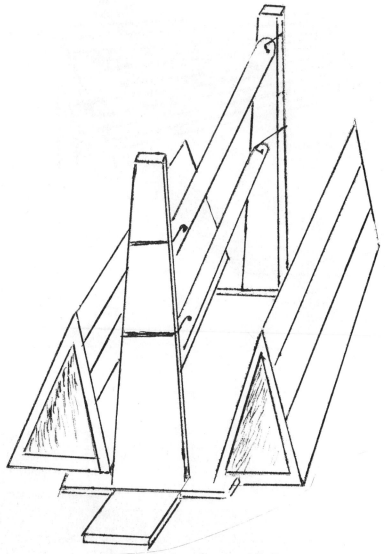

Double Chicken Coop and Rail.

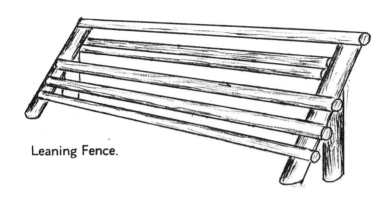

Leaning Fence.

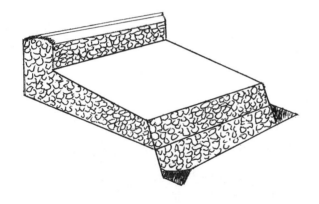

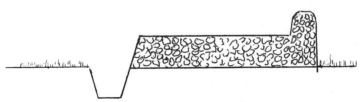

Piano Jump (bottom: profile).

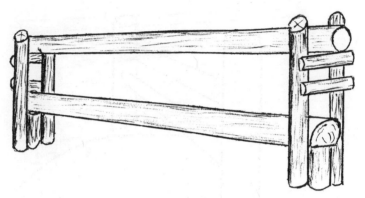

Telephone Pole.

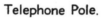

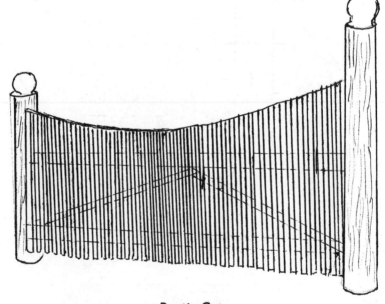

Rustic Gate.

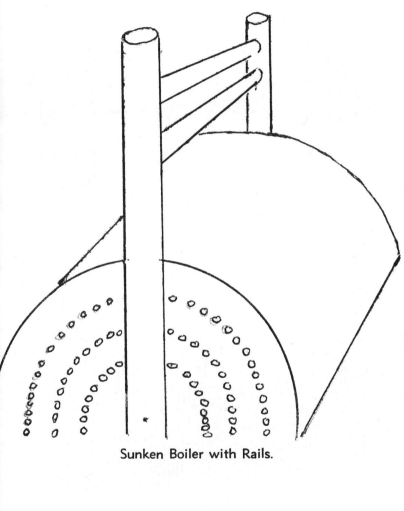

Sunken Boiler with Rails.

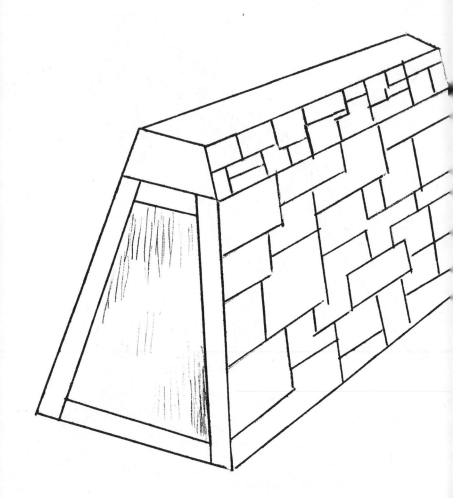

Stone Wall.

"Detour" Jump.

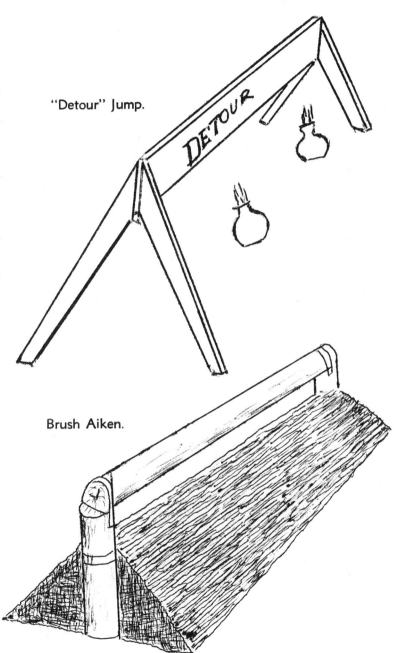

Brush Aiken.

12. Teaching Young Jumpers

The schooling of the young horse in jumping must never become one-sided. It must be administered in small doses, as an integral part of his general education. Too much emphasis on it may be just as harmful as too little, and the trainer's understanding of a horse's psychology is of the utmost importance.

If the schooling is handled correctly, particularly during the first critical days, the colt will look at a little jumping as good fun and kick up his heels in sheer joy of living. This is a spirit that never must be discouraged or replaced by fear. Care should be taken that the game is not continued beyond the first signs of tiredness and boredom, and

Beginner's Troubles.

the use of force or threats must be avoided. Keeping in mind that a horse, a young one in particular, is curious, timid and easily frightened, encouragement and gentle urging will soon prove to be more rewarding than bullying. A word of approval, a pat on the neck, a carrot, or a mouthful of grain following a good performance should become a habit never to be neglected. A horse is very sensitive to the tone of voice. He will recognize inflections of reassurance, firmness, gentleness, or anger and respond accordingly.

It is important that the young horse receives and retains the impression that the obstacles he is invited to negotiate are solid and that he can not push them over with his knees. Later on, of course, when the time comes for him to tackle higher and more dangerous barriers, the upper parts of them should be so constructed that heavy contact will knock them over. But even then, the respect for immovable obstacles will be remembered, having become part of his instincts.

Watching a jumper perform in the arena of a horse-show, it is not difficult to distinguish between those that have been trained in the proper manner and the not so fortunate ones. If his background is a nightmare of poling, whipping, or worse, he usually approaches an obstacle in what seems to be wild-eyed terror. Even if his habitual tormentor is missing this time, his attention will still instinctively be partly directed toward the spot where the man with the whip or the pole used to stand. A horse that has been trained along the principles of reward and patience presents a different picture. His approach gives the impression of deliberation and alert, confident concentration. He looks where he is going and can be counted on to cooperate, providing he understands what is required of him.

The best way to introduce a young horse to the business of jumping is to use solid poles, firmly wrapped with a

"Whoa!"

rope of twisted straw till they are a foot thick. This is
something that will not frighten him. At the same time
the poles look too solid to be kicked around, but they will
not hurt his legs if he should bump into them.

The colt should be introduced to these poles just as soon
as he has settled down to work at the end of a longe. To
begin with he is led by hand over a pole placed across the
track. He should be allowed to examine it and sniff at it
as much as he wants, until he steps across without urging.
Walking and trotting over the log follows, accompanied
by playful little jumps. Another similar pole may then be
placed across the track 12 feet or so from the first. The two
poles are left there, flat on the ground, until the colt is
thoroughly used to them. Then follows the slow process
of building a barrier, first with one pole, later with two
on top of each other, always keeping in mind that they
are solidly anchored. Flimsy and easily collapsible obstacles should at all cost be avoided.

It may seem that it hardly should be necessary to go

into so much detail in discussing the preliminary steps in
the schooling of a jumper. But the fact is that this period
usually is the most important part of his education and
too often neglected. While longeing should be used to
acquaint the horse with as many types of jumps as possible, the greatest care must be taken not to discourage
or frighten him by building them up too rapidly or making
them too easy to knock down.

Training in jumping ditches and other wide obstacles is
usually not practical by using the longe and can wait till
the horse is well advanced in his schooling under saddle.
If a fenced-in lane (previously described) is available,
ditches can be introduced at an earlier stage and to good
advantage. With or without rider "nightmare alley" is an
ideal place for a young horse to learn to adjust his stride
and speed and to gain experience in general, with nobody
to interfere. The alley should also include banks and piano
jumps with variations. They constitute the most valuable
forms of practice obstacles, helping to build muscles and
agility, for instance.

Another critical period of the schooling of the young
horse begins with the schooling under saddle. Another
element is then added to the many other problems. Is the
rider a well-educated horseman, able to be an experienced
help to his horse, or is he of the type that has to be helped
by the horse and handicaps his efforts in every way possible?

Obviously, no young horse in training should be asked
to do any jumping until he has found his balance with the
heavy weight on his back, thoroughly adjusted himself to
the new conditions and developed the muscular strength
that makes jumping possible. The routine of the first stage
must start all over again, right from the padded pole
across the track. The slower his progress is from then on,
the better. Impatience born of ignorance and commercial
considerations in this day and age usually make a tragic

joke out of the training of jumpers. Quick results are more important than good and honest results; short cuts are more valuable than humane decency when the goal is a blue ribbon; whipping and poling are the modern methods, but have so far failed to prove that they are more efficient than the old system of patience and reward—quite to the contrary if we are to judge by the performances at horseshows in recent years. An attempt to condition the horse by incessant jumping is another bad mistake. It is not by far the best way to develop his muscles, and chances are that he may lose his natural ambition and even turn "sour." When that happens, he will jump only because he is afraid of punishment.

Besides strong muscles, a good jumper also needs wind and endurance. Increasing periods of quiet gallops and walking up and down hill and jumping on and off banks are effective. In this connection I can not refrain from mentioning an evil and unnecessary custom at horseshows, where jumping is a too important part of the program. I am referring to the so-called "jump-offs." If two or more horses finish the course in a tie, they are put through an additional test that continues until all but one has been eliminated.

The participants in the jump-off are allowed no respite and a chance to catch their breath after finishing the course. They are immediately put to jumping a barrier that is moved up an inch or two at a time. Quite often they have to repeat the jump over and over again before the victor is decided. It is not unusual to have this go on until one or more of the animals collapses from exhaustion, gets seriously hurt, or even dies from over-exertion.

There would seem to be less primitive ways of solving a tie than measuring inches or fractions of inches with a tape measure on a fence. There are such things as the horse's manner of going over the course he has just passed and the rider's ability.

SUMMING UP

Any young horse who is bred for sports riding loves to jump; it is just another outlet for his exuberance. A horseman who understands this and has sense enough to use training methods that take advantage of a colt's courage and natural instincts will need no spiked poles, whips, electric shocks, or murderous spurs. A horse will perform better for an understanding friend than for a bully who depends on fear and punishment.

I recently had the doubtful pleasure of watching a young man getting his jumper ready for a horseshow. Coming out of the stable he circled the arena two or three times at a trot and canter. With no further limbering up the horse was put against a four-foot barrier, which he cleared clumsily. The horse was known as an excellent jumper and he passed the bar fluently the second time. But then the rider suddenly had the pole moved up from four to six feet. This was, of course, senseless, and the horse balked twice, in spite of freely applied spurs and whip. The third time he tried frantically, but hit the bar with his knees, floundered badly and ended up scratched and bleeding. Two days before I had watched this same horse clearing six feet with ease. But on that occasion he had been properly warmed up and the build-up from four to six feet had been gradual.

It should be obvious that it is vital for a jumper not only to be properly exercised and prepared for an effort as strenuous as jumping, but that he also is in condition to perform safely and with confidence.

By far the best kind of gymnastics for getting a jumper in shape, both as part of his training and for limbering up before a performance, is 30 to 60 minutes of the practical dressage movements previously described. If correctly executed, they will not only develop the muscle systems of back, croup and hindquarters, but will also improve the horse's ability to balance himself quickly and easily, with or without the rider's assistance, to meet the constantly changing needs of the jumping arena. Immediate response to the rider's guiding aids is another important product of elementary dressage.

Great care must, however, be taken that the "élan" of a good horse, his natural urge to move ahead, is not discouraged by too much use of calisthenics in the ring at slow gaits and tempo. In other words, the collecting exercises in the school ring must be alternated with free moving rides in the open. This is particularly important in the training of steeple-chasers and hunters, where stamina and wind are deciding qualities. The trainer should keep in mind, however, that the horse never should be allowed to "run himself out" during fast-gait exercises. He should be reined in while he is still raring to go.

The shaping of a good jumper requires an elaborate and intelligently applied system. Without it, his participation in shows, contests and exhibitions may become highly damaging abuse.

When a jumper balks, shies, or fumbles, the rider invariably seems to have an alibi all ready, and always to the effect that the horse was at fault. This understandable attitude fortunately does not very often lead to extremes similar to a recent occasion involving a young lady participating in a society horseshow.

I ran into her accidentally in a secluded corridor, where she was busily belaboring her horse's face with a hunting whip. She informed me that the villainous creature had "let her down" and failed to win the cup for her by being so miserably clumsy. An hour earlier I had suffered agonies, watching her ride the horse, who was a magnificent jumper and would have won the prize if the girl's lack of ability had given him a chance. Jumpers showing signs of balkiness, fear, excessive nervousness, or even blind panic are all pitiful products of brutal training methods. Pre-

vious experience has taught them to associate jumping
with punishment and pain. Half of their attention is dis-
tracted to one end or the other of the obstacle, where they
are used to seeing a frightening figure wielding a black-
snake whip, a pole, or some other contraption that they
know is going to hurt.

13. In the Open Field

A gallop across the open country offers a multitude of problems of many different kinds. Even in its mildest form it is a severe test both of horse and rider. A good horse may be able to drag the dead-weight rider—equipped with a whip and lots of conceit—through to the finish, but it will take more out of him than he can afford. He might have been spared at least half of the heavy going and still have made better time.

A good horseman knows instinctively how to adjust his speed according to the nature of the ground he is covering. He will not ride too fast across a pleasant, level meadow that invites full speed ahead. Instead he uses it to conserve his horse's strength for the long hill at the other end. Approaching this, the horse will want to make a rush and take advantage of his momentum to carry him as far up the incline as possible. All the rider needs to do is to give him his head, and if he knows his business, he will do just that, while he transfers his weight well forward over the withers. Downhill on the other side, the horse lowers his head to see where he is going, and the rider should give him enough rein for this purpose, without removing the reassuring support of the bit.

There may be hard stretches that might be damaging to feet and tendons. A slower tempo is then called for also to avoid slipping and falling. On a hard surface, the educated rider has a decided advantage, too; he can retain a faster tempo without danger or damage than the careless greenhorn, by gathering his horse up under him—collecting him.

It is a sensible precaution to take the feet out of the stirrups when passing creekbeds full of slippery rocks, swampy ground and similar rough spots where a horse may lose his footing. Occasions when it becomes necessary to swim with a horse do not occur frequently, but it can do no harm to know how to handle the situation. A horse is a fair swimmer and can be trusted to take care of himself in water if he is left alone. The rider should never remain in the saddle of a swimming horse. It should also be remembered that it is very easy to tip him over backwards. A jerk on the reins may be all it takes. It should further be kept in mind that he swims with his hindlegs paddling way up under his belly. The rider can swim beside him by holding on to the pommel, providing he remembers not to pull on the reins and to stay away from the forward reaching hindlegs. The best thing the rider can do is to slip back and let the horse pull him while he holds on to the tail. The horse needs no guidance to head in the right direction.

As far as fences, ditches and other obstacles are concerned the technique is in general the same as in the show ring, except that there will be a tendency to approach too fast, to neglect keeping the horse collected and to ride him actively all the time. To approach a fence with the horse's head pulled way up is asking for trouble. When a wide ditch is ahead, it is easy to forget that slight slowing down, followed immediately by a free rein, makes it possible for the hindlegs to get hold for their drive.

Point-to-point races used to be popular some time ago. Since they were as much a test of the rider's ability as of the stamina of the horse, they may be disappearing now, together with the knowledge of horsemanship. In these competitions the condition of the horse at the finish counts 50 percent and the performance both of horse and rider the remaining 50 percent. As a rule there is no credit for less time than the stipulated maximum.

Driving an automobile there is always a certain speed

that is the most economical. This is equally true on horseback. The only difference is that, when a horse is involved, the most favorable tempo varies constantly with the contour of the terrain.

A young lady who was a conscientious reader of the society column had come across the word "drag hunt" in connection with certain activities involving red coats and horses. Being only 12 years old and unsophisticated, she was curious about the "drag" part and whether it had anything to do with the rider. Since I am a firm believer in strict adherence to the truth when children seek information about the facts of life, I explained as diplomatically as I could that this indeed frequently was the case. A few pounds more or less do not mean as much to the horse as how the weight is distributed. One of the world's most famous steeple-chase riders weighed 220 pounds.

Frequent and careless changes and adjustments of weight and position must be avoided. It takes very little to disturb the balance of a horse trying to concentrate his attention on the next obstacle and throw him off stride. It will also destroy his confidence and distract him. Fiddling with the reins is all it takes to produce a stumble on uneven ground or at a jump. Regardless of how good a rider is, or thinks he is, he should not be allowed to take a horse out of the stable unless he has at least a fair conception of how much it can stand without being abused. Sweating and respiration are useful guides, but far from conclusive. Abuse can begin long before breathing turns into painful panting. Some horses have more endurance and stamina than others and each horse must be judged on his own merits. The cross-country part of the three-day event of the Olympic Games probably represents the utmost limits to which a horse's endurance can be stretched. This test requires a horse with outstanding natural qualities, usually trained by the person who rides him in the event and who himself must have a thorough schooling as a horseman. Like his horse, he must be in prime condition.

The cross-country takes place on the second of the three days. The extremely varied course covers about 22½ miles and the total time allowed is two hours, five minutes, and six seconds. It is divided into three main parts. The first is over roads and paths for four and one-half miles, with a time allowance of 29 minutes and 10 seconds. No credit is given for using less time. The second main part is the steeple-chase, two and one-half miles long. The time allowed is six minutes and 40 seconds. Credit is given for undertime in this phase. The third and main part, immediately following the steeple-chase, is the actual cross-country. This part is again divided into three phases, the first being nine and one-half miles over roads and paths in one hour and two and one-half minutes. No credit is allowed for using less time. The second phase follows at once—five miles cross country over 30 to 40 severe natural obstacles. This is the hardest part of the test and few survive it without heavy penalties. This phase has a bonus for undertime. The time allowed is 17 minutes and 46 seconds. After these five miles there is a gallop of one and one-quarter miles to the finish in six minutes and five seconds. There is no bonus for undertime, but trotting disqualifies.

In the 1964 Olympic Games in Tokyo the United States Equestrian team collected six silver medals and, among other honorable feats, placed second in the grueling three-day event. This is something to be proud of, considering the sorry state of existing equestrian standards.

It was not easy to get this information. I tried two local libraries first without success. Next, I asked the sports editor of a metropolitan newspaper. He said he had no dope on it and obviously could not be bothered looking up an item of so little interest to the public. He helpfully suggested, however, that "maybe the society editor. . . ."

In desperation I wrote to two of the slickest sports magazines. One of them sent back a postcard with two lines typed on it to the effect that they were too busy to do any research. The other was a little more obliging, and while they regretted having no information on the subject, they gave me the address of the Olympic Committee, who promptly mailed me a printed publication containing the results of the games in detail. Newspapers and sports magazines can not be blamed, I suppose, for limiting themselves to subjects that they feel are of interest to their readers, but it does not seem unreasonable to expect that a sport, recognized as an important part of the Olympic Games right from their international conception, should not be ignored and brushed off as a society caper.

It is true enough that newspapers seem to have been less reluctant of late in printing news concerning riding activities not related to racing, and horse magazines are getting bigger and glossier all the time. But since they are mostly interested in fads, they contribute little to promote knowledge or even simple understanding of good horsemanship. Efforts to improve the breed of the many types of horses is important and seem to be successful, but I fail to see how page after page listing the ancestors and relatives (stud book fashion) of some equine celebrity can be of public interest.

Nobody tries to disguise the fact that all these improvement activities aim at producing race horses that can run faster and show horses that can step higher, the benefit to the public being limited to losing money by betting on them or spending money for the privilege of admiring them in the show ring. There can be no doubt that full-page pictures of cow girls in emerald stretch pants is good business, but they can be of little help to the growing hordes of horseback riders. I cannot help but feel that publications that deal exclusively with horses and related subjects should not only be aware of the fact that the equitation events are among the most prominent in the Olympic Games. They should also explain what they consist of, how horses and riders are trained, and who the riders and instructors are. Something about the breed and family trees of the horses might also be of interest to many people. Information of this nature would have important educational value, which is more than can be said about the oceans of idiotic fads that threaten to confuse and destroy all sound conceptions of horsemanship.

14. On the Trail, Bridle Path and Road

Since the following is still meant to be a discussion of good horsemanship under varying conditions, the trails mentioned are of the kind that are constructed for riding, not climbing. The sublime pleasure of handling a fine horse is the primary purpose; the scenery is secondary, and transportation along precipitous mountain trails does not enter into it at all. Neither do I have in mind an image of Hoot Gibson, Jr., loping along, rocking-chair fashion, "tall in the saddle," shoulders on the level of the ears, hands just below the chin.

My aim is to call attention to a few things that decide the difference between an enjoyable ride and a dull one, with no other purpose than a little exercise. Even more important to a horseman, worthy of the title, is to know how to handle his horse in such a way that his strength and endurance are not abused on a long ride. An ignorant or sloppy rider can turn a few hours on a pleasant trail into an ordeal for the horse. He will remember it next time and show an increasing lack of enthusiasm for leaving the stable.

Inspection of saddling and bridling should be routine. Also take a look at feet and legs. A loose shoe, a small rock, a hot hoof, or tendon may mean a long walk home. Make it a rule even if you ride a familiar horse to make contact with boots and reins as soon as you are settled in the saddle, and do not allow the contact with the boots to be interrupted as long as you stay on the horse. He should be aware of and attentive to the boots even during relaxation periods. The rhythmical, alternate application of the boots at a walk will help to lengthen the stride, and their use when posting, as previously explained, will have the same effect and enforce more efficient action.

The first ten minutes after mounting should be used to limber up the horse at a brisk walk with long reins. The trot should not be started till full control has been established by gathering up the reins. Only when he is fully collected and light in the hand, and when his hindlegs are well under, should he be allowed to start trotting. It is important that the horse never be permitted to change from a slower to a faster gait without being under full control and in the proper form. The increase of tempo should be easy and gradual. An unprepared, sudden rush is always an unnecessary effort for the horse, and can lead to trouble. Attention to small details like these may seem of little practical value and slightly ridiculous to the horseman who wants results in a hurry. But the fact is that the accumulation of many such "silly" precautions always adds up to some form of serious mistreatment that sooner or later will produce its effects. This may explain why so many fine horses are sent back to the trainer for "retraining"—an entirely new procedure that saves the owner from the old-fashioned and tiresome necessity of learning to ride himself.

Always ride with both hands on the reins. During rest periods with the reins loose, it is advisable to take all reins in the left hand and the slack in the right. You are then prepared to pull them tight quickly and retain control without fumbling if the horse is frightened or suddenly attempts some independent action.

You should sit the trot the first few beats to make sure that your mount is balanced the way he should be. Make mental note of which diagonal you are posting and remember to use the other in the next period of trot.

Trot should be used only where the path is level or slopes gently upwards. It can, however, also be maintained on very slight downgrades, providing the horse is checked to a little slower tempo and is well collected. On a level track, 10 to 15 minutes of trot, interrupted by five minutes of relaxation, has proved to be the best plan. At a tempo of eight miles an hour the trot can under favorable conditions be kept up for 30 minutes at a time, providing it is steady and regular. It is the most efficient speed because it will combine the best mileage within the shortest time with the smallest expenditure of energy. In other words, you make the best progress with the least wear and tear on your horse. Trotting eight miles an hour on a level track will not accelerate your horse's respiration or make him sweat even in warm weather if he is in normal condition. In fact, an overheated horse can be cooled off at this rate of speed, and his respiration reduced to normal.

An extended trot is never used on the trail, but a fast canter can be allowed when approaching a steep hill (to take advantage of the momentum), except when hard surface forbids a fast gait. An occasional slow canter where surface and grade are favorable will help to relax a horse and should be used on long rides, but always sparingly; and under no circumstances must it become the standard gait. Canter must never be done downhill, even if the incline is very slight, or uphill at any time. If in doubt, watch your horse's breathing.

A short trip on a pleasant bridle path is, of course, something else again. While there are individuals who can half kill a horse in less than an hour and plead afterwards that they did not know they were doing anything wrong (which probably would be an honest statement at that), there can be no objection to longer periods of canter when circumstances do not demand careful observance of economy in regard to the horse's strength and endurance.

It must be clearly understood, however, that the "long rides" that are the subject of our discussion, have no relation to the "100-mile cup races" that are becoming so popular in the West. They belong among subjects only distantly connected with horsemanship and will be analyzed later.

As already mentioned, the steady, machine-like tempo is a fundamental principle among the rules and regulations governing rides of a full day's duration or more. It refers to every gait and tempo. A horse can cover a mile at a steady, well-regulated speed with less effort than a fraction of that distance at an irregular, constantly changing pace. This is also true if the different gaits are mixed up every few minutes, aimlessly without plan, rhyme, or reason. In regard to the eight miles an hour standard tempo of trot one young equestrienne sensibly objected that since her horse was not equipped with a speedometer, how was she to know whether he was doing 8 or 18. The best answer I am able to give is that if judgment of tempo has not been drilled into a student in the school ring, the next best thing is to give the matter a little serious attention during undisturbed moments on the bridle path. Every horse has a tempo of his own in which he seems to be more at ease and move with less effort. By feeling his way, any rider with some experience will soon find the right tempo, and from then on all he has to do is to keep it steady.

A regular tempo can not be maintained effectively without the active assistance of the rider. He can not afford to relax the control of his mount's rate of speed or form even for short periods. He can not allow himself to rest while his horse works, and his job becomes more strenuous as the horse grows tired and begins to drift with the forehand gradually taking over more of the carrying. When the delicate balance between boots and bit, that is the key to economy of action, begins to fall apart, the stimulation of a gentle spur point may become necessary, like a "shot in the arm." The use of a whip on a tired horse is an act of brutality and does nothing but harm; a spur properly used is humane, merciful and effective.

A horse's feet are vulnerable and can easily be hurt or damaged even if they are shod. Joints and tendons suffer from the same weakness, particularly the ones in the front legs. Prolonged pounding on hard surfaces will have disastrous results, and no faster gait than a walk should be permitted on pavement, and even then for very short periods. Hard gravel roads can be just as bad, and loose rocks will be more harmful than cement. Pavement is also preferable to the shoulder of the road if this is muddy and slippery. A good bridle path should be soft, but firm and springy. Loose sand and soggy ground should be avoided and the rider must never neglect to keep a watchful eye ahead and guide his horse around holes, rocks, or anything else that may cause him to stumble or hurt his feet.

Upon the first indication of lameness dismount immediately and locate the source of the trouble. It is advisable always to carry along a large nail to clean out the soles of the hooves. If a shoe should have come loose, it is better to remove it.

If the trouble is a hot tendon and there is water available, temporary relief can be obtained by letting him stand in it for an hour at least.

Among horsemen there has always been a rule, accepted as a matter of course, that the horse should be attended to before the rider. When you are on a full day's ride and stop in the middle of the day for a bite to eat, look after your horse first. Take the saddle off and give his back a good rubbing. Do not forget, before you put blanket and saddle back on, to brush the ruffled hair until it is smooth, as a precaution against saddle sores.

To prevent him from having colic, do not let him drink too fast when he is warm and very thirsty. To slow down the intake, leave the bridle on or let him sip the water through a handful or two of hay or straw placed in the bucket. Feed him as soon as he is dry, at ease and comfortable. Returning to the stable, walk the horse the last ten minutes. If he still should be warm, dismount and lead him until he has cooled off and his respiration is normal.

It may seem superfluous to keep harping on these old rules that have been stated and repeated so many times before, but judging by the common neglect in observing them, they are badly in need of being rubbed in all over again.

The motto of modern times being what it is—to do things with the least possible effort—the incessant activity in the saddle, prescribed even for a ride on the trail, may never become popular. But the few who have learned how find it very much worth while. It constitutes the difference between being a horseman and a passenger.

15. Voltige

Before the student can settle down to active riding he must be mentally as well as physically relaxed and have acquired a dependable sense of balance. One of the quickest and most effective ways to create the confidence that makes this possible is to relieve the monotony of class routine with periods of voltige. In its milder forms these exercises are beneficial also for older people, regardless of experience. For youngsters, from 12 years upwards, they are lots of fun and highly rewarding. They can be adapted to flat saddles, with or without stirrups, or a blanket fastened with a girth. For the more acrobatic stunts a specially constructed voltige girth is necessary.

To begin with you are introduced to a placid and somewhat corpulent horse without any visible backbone. There is no saddle or even a blanket. Instead there is a padded and solid-looking strap with two suitcase handles sticking up one on each side of the withers. There is also a rein on each side, running from the rings of a snaffle bit and secured to the girth, serving as a kind of tie-down to keep his head in the right position. A long line is tied to the chin strap and is held by the instructor, who stands in the center of a big circle in one end of the arena with a long whip in his other hand to keep the horse moving on the track.

The horse is trained to a slow, rocking-horse canter that feels very comfortable, and you have the two reassuring handles within easy reach, so you take a deep breath and relax. You cross your arms on your chest and kick your legs nonchalantly.

Even if your previous athletic feats have rarely passed

the bending-an-elbow and stepping-on-the-gas-pedal stage, you may feel your latent recklessness soar, to the extent that you attempt swinging a leg over the horse's neck and end up sitting sideways, still with your arms crossed. After executing this successfully with both legs alternately a few times, you may become over-confident, loose your balance, and gently slide off your slippery perch. At least your instructor hopes you will, not because he is a sadistic brute, but because he wants you to find out that the distance down to the sawdust is not as fearsome as it seems and that no danger is involved.

How to proceed from there depends on the aptitude of the individuals. Most of them can be persuaded to go on from the sideways position to hoist a leg over the rump (the horse's) and end up facing backwards. For various reasons this somewhat informal seat will create frightening and confusing sensations and the student is usually more than willing to complete his 360-degree tailspin and return to a normal position. Another stunt consists of relaxing completely in a horizontal position, laying down flat on your back. There are also any number of bendings and twistings possible, as prescribed by the Swedish manuals of gymnastics, that will do wonders for elderly athletes of both sexes and have the advantage that they will not interfere with the equilibrium.

The "Scissors" is something else again. They require agility and the conviction that the sawdust is a pleasant landing place—until you get the knack of it, that is. The details of this operation are as follows:

1. Take hold of the suitcase handles with an underhand grip and place your elbows in a carrying position under your ribs.
2. Lean strongly forward until your full weight rests on your hands and elbows and your seat is lifted an inch or so from the horse.

3. For practice, swing your legs back and up as far as you can, click your heels and return to where you were.
4. Swing the legs back and up again, but instead of clicking your heels, cross your legs before you hit the horse again with your left leg on his right side and the right on the left side. You will then find yourself facing backwards.
5. Return to normal position in the same manner, except that the croup is used to lean on instead of the handles. It is easier than you might think.

Your objection to the "On-And-Off" may be that you are no acrobat and have no intention to join a circus. Actually it is not as difficult as it looks. I have with my own eyes seen a 72-year-old senior citizen execute it smoothly, without harm to his heart condition.

Before you go into action, the instructor will encourage the horse into somewhat livelier action. The faster he canters the easier the performance becomes. When you feel that he has reached a satisfactory speed, accompanied by a more vigorous lift of the back, your right leg is swung across to the left side. Simultaneously the left hand takes a firm over-hand hold of the left handle, and the right hand an underhand grip on the left. The legs are stretched down and forward in jumping off. If you descend in step with the horse, your feet will touch the ground well in front of the shoulder and you will bounce right back like a rubber ball in one fluid motion.

16. Mailed Fist Under Silken Glove

My discussion of things like "curbs," "spurs," "whips" and "martingales," is meant as a warning, just as the rack and the thumb screw and the atom bomb emphasize the advantage of staying on the straight and narrow path. They are murderous in the hands of ignorant, overly emotional, or brutal individuals. In the sensitive hands of a good horseman they are valuable assets. A horse's education is not completed until his obedience to the aids is instinctive and his response has become second nature. An ignorant rider on a well-trained horse is no better off than a tourist in a foreign country where he can not make himself understood. A similar impasse is the result of a reversed situation.

Nevertheless, a good horseman cannot afford to leave anything to chance. He knows that situations may arise when he must assert his authority. But he also knows that punishment is the last resort and should be avoided. A warning given firmly and with understanding is more effective. A horse should at all times respect his rider as the boss, but never be afraid of him.

THE CURB

There are only two kinds of standard bridling that experience has proved to be the most practical as well as the most humane: One is the snaffle used alone, the other is snaffle and mild curb used together. The curb should never be used alone. It is ineffective as an instrument of guidance unless the principle of control is the use of force.

It may seem less than charitable to put more than one

bit in a horse's sensitive mouth and it hardly would seem necessary. It is quite true that if the bits are not adjusted with the utmost care and handled the same way, they can turn the mouth into a bloody mess. But in the hands of a good rider this combination of bits has important advantages and to the horse they are meant to be a blessing in disguise.

While the active guiding of the horse is done with the snaffle, the curb is passive. The curb reins should be given constant attention and frequently adjusted to prevent them from becoming too tight. The delicate play of hands and fingers will cause the two bits to roll gently against each other. The horse will react by chewing on them, and when he does that, the muscles in his neck and jaw will relax. This flexing is, as mentioned before, the key to easy handling and control.

To inexperienced riders, the danger of a run-away horse is always present and very real. He will usually start by leaning heavily on the bit with a stiff neck. "He takes the bit in his teeth." Violent use of the curb will then have no effect except damaging his mouth and increasing his frenzy. All this may be avoided if the flexing is maintained at all times. This is the real purpose of the curb: supporting the snaffle and preventing the horse from taking hold of the bit.

The curb bit should be placed below the snaffle in the horse's mouth and must not touch the teeth. The chain will pass below the snaffle so that it does not interfere with the free action of this bit. It should be twisted carefully until it is perfectly flat, and be long enough to allow the arms of the curb to form an angle of 45 degrees with the horse's lips when the reins are gently tightened. The shorter the chain is and the lower in the horse's mouth the bit is placed, the more severe the effect of the curb will become.

THE SPURS

It can not be denied that spurs are very impressive in their effect on the non-riding hoi-polloi, particularly if they jingle and glitter and have rowels the size of silver dollars and teeth sharp as needles. Their effect on a horse is something else again.

There are spurs in every shape and form, some that can tear a horse's flanks to shreds, some that are not meant to have any effect at all. Some are designed for show, others for brutal punishment.

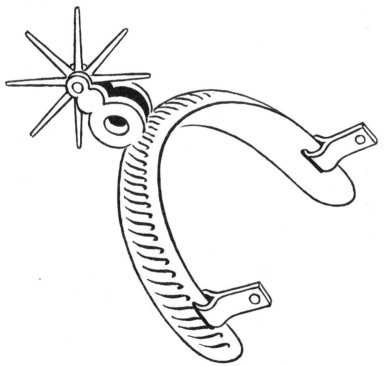

The "Mexican" Spur, an instrument of torture.

There is only one model, with minor variations, that has been generally accepted as practical and effective, without being harmful to the horse or dangerous to the rider. This is the English hunting spur, also called dressage spur, with small rowels and short teeth. It is constructed to create respect without harming, to enforce obedience without abuse. A light touch with the spur is usually enough to ensure quick response, and avoid sluggish re-action to the boots as well as wear and tear on the rider's legs.

As soon as a horse becomes aware of the presence of the spurs they need be applied very rarely, unless he is very tired. In that case, regular pin-pricks with the spurs will serve a double purpose: prevent slowing down and counteract the slackening of the muscles that leads to inefficiency of action and reduced endurance.

Some horses will resist the spurs by kicking or leaning against them. Others are so afraid of them that they panic at the mere suspicion of their presence. Both types are results of mistakes by riders who should not have been permitted to decorate themselves with spurs in the first place. The cure consists of patiently and methodically trying to convince the horse that he will never again be hurt that way, but that it nevertheless is safer to obey commands.

The "safe" horses, the backbone of the riding academy business, have learned to accept mistreatment for so long that they hardly react at all to the spurs. This does not mean that they are not hurt. It is only a kind of hopeless resignation. Obviously, nobody should be allowed to use spurs until they are at least in full control of their own movements in the saddle. There are all too many riders of this category that should be barred from wearing this badge of the expert horseman because of their temper, temperament and mental attitude in general. There used to be a dogma that was taken very seriously by horsemen

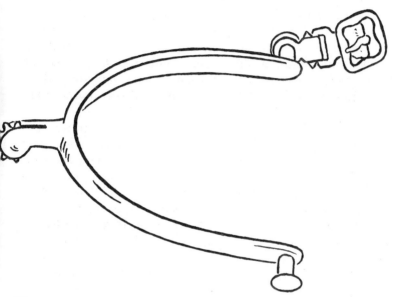

The Most Humane Spur, practical in any form of riding.

of a bygone age: the points of the spurs should be as sensitive as your fingertips and you should always be fully aware whether the rowels only ruffle the hair of your horse's flank or actually touch the skin.

If spurs have to be used, they should be used with discretion and level-headed evalution of the situation at hand.

THE WHIP

As is the case with the spurs, the purpose of the whip is to enforce respect for and obedience to the three main aids—weight, boots and reins. Carried in a full grip in the right hand, it will not interfere with the manipulation of the reins. For warning and animating it should be used only on the shoulder, which it can reach easily by a slight twist of the wrist. If it must be applied to overcome balkiness, it should be used immediately behind the right boot while all reins are gathered in the left hand. Under no circumstance should the whip be used in any other way or in any other place.

Today, when so many horses are "broken" and whiptrained in 30 days, where we old-time slow-pokes could not do it in less than two or three years, many horses start their career being afraid of whips. The danger of waving it around too much should be impressed on the beginner, as well as the reasons why it should be kept quietly in one place.

To the inexperienced horseman the whip is both safer and more effective than the spurs, and the student should get used to carrying it from the beginning.

THE MARTINGALE

The purpose of the martingale is to prevent the horse from getting out of control by carrying or throwing his head too high. There are two kinds of martingales: the standing and the running. The standing martingale, or tie-down, does not allow the horse to raise his head above a certain fixed position. It can not be adjusted while riding. It is used extensively in polo and by working cowboys where quick action is required and sudden and violent use of the reins can not always be avoided.

For all other forms of riding the running martingale is preferable. It should be used in connection with a snaffle only and two pairs of reins, one of which runs through the rings of the martingale and is used in the same manner as the curb reins. Since it can be regulated during the ride, the running martingale is gentle in its action.

PART II

A Glimpse Behind the Scenes

17. Rough Stuff

The study of the finer points of dressage requires a certain amount of intellectual effort that may lead to a mental strain, and a diversion at this time to subjects easier to digest and closer to home seems to be called for to provide a moment of relaxation.

A lady of my acquaintance has not only been interested in horses all her life but has also suffered from a chronic and unquenchable thirst for knowledge pertaining to equitation. She went to one instructor after another, trying to get at the truth. They all disagreed with each other on everything, with one exception: the others were phonies and didn't know what they were talking about. She belonged to horsy organizations whose members did not need their arms twisted to make them admit that they were experts and both willing and able to offer helpful advice to a friend.

The lady finally had to recognize the fact that she was making no progress whatsoever in her study of horsemanship. She broke all connections with associations and the most insistent of her well-meaning friends, and bought herself a horse. This is perhaps better expressed by saying that somebody sold her a horse. I have never seen it, but she described it as "a nice little Palomino." She further explained that for the time being he was in the hands of a "most capable trainer." The next report I received was that the time had finally come for the trainer to allow her to ride her horse. In spite of her brave attempt to smile delightedly, she later admitted the fact that she had been unable to get her "nice little Palomino" to move faster than a slow walk. To be truthful, she had had trouble keeping him moving at all, and could I please loan her a pair of spurs? After that I heard nothing from her for a long time. I finally made inquiries and found out that she had a broken arm; she was unable to report by mail and was not permitted to drive a car. She had fallen off her "nice little Palomino" the first time she tried him after the trainer's assurance that all his bad habits had been cured. According to her, he moved willingly enough this time, but had suddenly stuck his head down between his legs and bucked her off. Having learned from experience, I offered my condolences but refrained from advice.

The level of education in horsemanship seems to be on its way down, and the horseback riding public depends more and more on the trainers. Their main objective is to break the spirit of the horses left in their hands so completely that the greenest of riders can handle (or abuse) them safely. Generally speaking, they seem to be succeeding admirably. Most of the horses you see around the country side are beautiful, well-bred animals, but they seem to be only half alive. There is no prancing and snorting and eager alertness. They are dragging their feet, unless they are forced by whip and spurs into an artificial show of high spirits.

The methods used by trainers are usually influenced by the urgency of getting quick results, and even the most competent of them may be forced to resort to ways and means that will result in irreparable damage. Quite frequently the outcome will be something like the "nice little Palomino" described before. The young lady felt that her experience was an instructive example of life among the horsy set and gave me an unabridged report of her misadventures.

The mare was said to be four years old at the time but was suspected of being younger than that. This means that she was worked, and worked hard, under saddle long

before a colt's bones are set and able to stand the strain.
This is the young lady's story:

She had been spoiled by extreme cruelty to begin with,
followed by a period of too easy handling. She had decided
that she could bluff her way out of working, and bucking
was one way of doing it.

They told me at the stable that her first owner was a big,
heavy man, who just wanted her to run and run all the time.
He wanted to train her as a roping horse. She is very small,
not much bigger than a big pony, does not have the conformation, speed, or temperament for that kind of work.
She was beaten into a state of dopey resignation. This was
what fooled me, I couldn't believe that a three year old
could be so calm and docile, but the vet said that she still
had her baby teeth. However, what I took for calmness
under saddle soon turned out to be just a sign that she had
given up fighting blindly and that she had learned to wait
for a favorable opportunity to get even with her tormentor.

The man finally just left her by simply not paying her
board to the stable, who then sold her to the second owners.
They went overboard in well-meant kindness, which did
more harm than good. The mare is sweet-acting, nickers to
everyone, and is easy to groom.

The new owners were even more ignorant than I am, and
she began to get away with everything, without opposition.
The moment she humped her back a little, tentatively, they
would immediately get off and lead her back to her stall.
She caught on to this right away and her life from then on
consisted of sugar cubes, grooming, and no riding.

She still had her terror of a male, however, as a result of
the abuse by the first owner, and when the son of the family
rode her on rare occasions, she would submit in a doped
kind of way. They took this for gentleness, as I did. They
finally decided to sell her and gave as the reason her small
size. They wanted a bigger horse. I later found out the real
reason—she had caught on to the family heir's lack of ability
as a horseman and dumped him too often.

Horse traders are the direct descendants of the pirates of

the Spanish Main—and I do not mean that as a compliment! The picture would not be complete without the ever-present lady friend, who has somehow talked herself into the unshakable conviction that there is nothing she does not know about training, handling and riding horses. One of them was right at my elbow, brimming over with expert advice. She offered to train the mare for me, so she would be absolutely safe and give me the confidence I seemed to lack. After that, she knew about "something" better that she would arrange for me to buy.

My expert lady friend rode my horse ONCE. She bucked, backed into a wall and refused to budge. That was the end of the schooling. She recommended a professional trainer to take over from there. "He is paid for getting clobbered!"

Naturally, she knew immediately that she was up against somebody who could not be trifled with, a trainer, and acted accordingly. She tried to buck with him, but he "just rode it out and then LET HER HAVE IT!"

When I went up there and rode her, she acted like a lady, but I realize now that the reason for this was that she was in constant view of the trainer. She watched him all the time. I was a mere dummy in the saddle.

So, the mare came back home, supposedly all trained. I should have had sense enough to know that all the cruelty could not be forgotten that easily. She received the best of care, but retained her sleepy look and attitude. She was well aware that I was leery of her and took full advantage of it. You could hardly blame her—she had been thoroughly convinced early in life, while she still was a baby, that a human was an enemy.

Under the circumstances it was difficult to give her the regular exercise she badly needed, and with one thing and another I suppose the final debacle was unavoidable. As soon as I got in the saddle, she started shying. I hung on. Then her head went down between her knees and on the second buck we parted company. She wandered over to the side of the ring to nibble some green grass; I was left sitting in the saw dust holding a broken arm and mumbling something un-lady-like in relation to expert advisors, trainers and phonies in general.

Instead of being reduced into abject slaves by having the courage and resistance beaten out of them, some horses will turn "sour." The treatment to which they have been submitted has killed their friendly instincts and left only a mixture of fear and hate toward their human tormentors. The "breaking" process has backfired, but it seemingly does not occur to anybody to blame the trainer and his methods. The moral is that an abused horse is never safe. Under the circumstances it is to be expected that accidents will occur. The only way to avoid them is to learn to ride properly. But even greenhorns have at least a chance to save their necks in emergencies by a few tricks that are directly connected with expert horsemanship. A safe type of saddle, for instance, can be important, not to mention the bit.

Several years ago I had a friend who was the proud owner of a horse that could be described only as an "outlaw." He would rear and buck and try to bolt. It was a typical example of a spirited horse turned bad by mistreatment. My friend had to suffer the consequences of somebody else's sins.

During an exhibition of rearing and bucking the horse finally went over backwards and fell on top of the rider, who escaped with a few broken ribs and a week in the hospital. A few weeks earlier I had succeeded in persuading him to replace his Western saddle with a flat, English model. He has never forgotten that he owes his life to this fact. The horn of a Western would have pierced his chest and killed him.

During my visit to a Texas ranch I was wondering why some of the boys occasionally carried loaded six-shooters. They explained that if they were thrown by a bolting horse and were dragged with one foot caught in the stirrup, there might be only one way to save their lives— shoot the horse.

It is easy to have a foot slip through the wide, wooden stirrups of a Western saddle, but not always so easy to get it out. Besides, the older models are not equipped with the safety lock of the English saddle, that automatically releases the stirrup if a backwards pull is exerted.

SHYING AND RUNNING AWAY

A frightened horse can get the best of us into a lot of trouble. Running away is one of the most serious things that may happen. There are several reasons for a horse's getting out of control and bolting. Something may actually have scared him, of course, or he may have felt frisky and in need of giving his exuberance an outlet by a little innocent cavorting that was misunderstood by the rider and that scared *him* out of his wits with predictable results. It must be admitted that there are horses who are just plain ornery and smart enough to recognize and take advantage of a rider's lack of experience. And who can blame them? Quite often this lack of experience will frighten and annoy a horse until he is driven to seek relief in flight. Heavy bumps in the saddle, sudden jerks on the reins or kicks with the boots, insecure balance or constant changes of position for other reasons may have a disastrous influence on the behavior of a good horse. Young horses in particular will sense if a person is afraid or nervous. They are quick to detect any tension and are not easily fooled by attempts to control and disguise an excited inflexion of voice or similar manifestations of non-existent confidence.

The instinctive reaction of an inexperienced or timid rider is to pull on the reins with a strength born of terror and to clutch frantically with his legs the moment he feels he is about to lose control. He will also seek safe anchorage

To stop run-away horse: Clutch reins hard in position shown and pull back.

This horse is supposed to be out of control. The rider must get off in a hurry. To avoid falling on his head, he grabs the horse firmly around the neck, and slides off.

by digging his heels into the horse's ribs. He does not have time to think logically and realize how senseless it is to accept a fight that he can not win. If he had kept his head, loosened instead of pulling on the reins, remained relaxed instead of having hysterical fits, he would at least have a chance to gain time to organize his defences.

It is difficult to prescribe a standard procedure to prevent a horse from bolting out of control. Realization of the cause of the trouble and timely anticipation, together with confident knowledge of how to handle the situation, gives the experienced horseman a deciding advantage. He will know, for instance, that a frightened horse must be treated differently from a malicious one, that there is a time for gentleness and soft talk and another for stern measures. He will never use a curb on a horse who is honestly afraid and he will resort to it only if everything else fails even on an "outlaw."

Inexperienced riders who can not be trusted with a curb anyway must use other means to save their necks, and there are fortunately a few tricks that may be successful and worth trying.

A horse preparing to bolt will usually start by trying to get hold of the bit. If he is successful, he takes it in his teeth, stretches his neck out stiff as a board, and away we go. All this can happen so fast that the rider has no time to act or even to think. To prevent the horse from getting hold of the bit at this moment may not stop him, but it will at least remove the support by the bit that a frantic pull on the reins would give him. Violent and panicky use of the reins may also result in pulling the head up into a position that makes it impossible for the horse to see where he is going and for the rider to get hold of him for more deliberate attempts at bringing him under control.

Sometimes a see-saw with the bit is all it takes to stop him, particularly if a snaffle is used. The effect of other kinds of bit is more brutal and the pain they inflict may aggravate the situation.

Short pulls followed by loosenings on both reins simultaneously, applied rhythmically at the exact moment when the frontfeet are off the ground, is another method worth trying if your biceps are not too atrophied.

If everything else fails, there is always one last recourse: Shorten the snaffle reins in the left hand until it is as close to the ears as you can reach. Then grip them firmly so that they will not slip between your fingers and pull the hand back along the crest. This will at least partially cut off the horse's breath and force him to slow down.

All of these methods are, of course, practicable only for reasonably experienced and able-bodied riders. In case these qualifications are lacking, it is much better to get out of the saddle as quickly as possible, before the horse gets into full stride. The safest and most practical way to dismount in a hurry is done this way: Get the feet clear of the stirrups and drop the reins. Lie down flat on your stomach, grab the horse firmly around the neck with both arms and hang on. Swing the right leg over, stretch your feet and legs as far forward as you can and let go with your arms. You may take a tumble when you land, but serious harm is as a rule avoided. It has been my experience that a safety measure of this kind should be practiced as a standard part of the drill in classes for youngsters.

BUCKING

For some reason or other bucking seems to be an inbred and common habit of Western horses. You can not help feeling that they have inherited and developed for generations an instinctive dislike for human beings and a deep-rooted suspicion of them that can have been caused only by mistreatment. At any rate, it pays to handle them with a certain circumspection at all times and keep this eccentricity of his in mind.

Other breeds will occasionally buck, too, and the best way to handle it is to learn to take it in your stride and hang on the best you can till he gets tired of it. All he wants is to get rid of you and if he fails, he will subside quickly. There is not much you can do to stop him anyway after he gets his head down between his front legs and his back up. There are, however, certain things you can do to reduce the odds against his getting started in the first place. Extra care should be taken in putting the saddle on and particularly in tightening the girth. It is a good idea to lead him around a minute or two before mounting and then let yourself down in the saddle slowly and smoothly, while you keep his head well up until you feel him relax.

BALKING

There are, of course, several reasons why a horse will balk, refuse to advance and to obey the aids. Whatever the cause is, it never pays to attack him suddenly and violently with boots, whip, or spurs. Patient but increasingly insistent use of the boots and, above all, a heavy, driving seat will usually overcome his resistance, but care must be taken not to increase his fright or excitement. Hammering with the boots and leaning forward at the same time will prove less than effective. If the whip has to be used, apply it with determination immediately behind the boot—not on the shoulder.

REARING

Rearing frequently accompanies balking and must be accepted passively by the rider. He can not do much about it except avoid pulling on the reins. If he tries to use the reins to save his own balance, he may make the horse fall over backwards. If this should happen, it is always the rider's own fault. Providing the horse does not have a "crew-cut" or is decorated for a horse show with those little tufts and ribbons along the crest, it is a better idea to hang on to the mane and let him rear until he gets tired of it.

18. Manners—Good and Bad

The rules of good behavior on horseback have one thing in common with those applying to the driver of an automobile—they are of a practical nature. They are safety measures, not only a display of good manners as another symptom of advanced culture.

One rule dating back to the age of chivalry is to pass another rider, coming in the opposite direction, with the right side against him. This is still practiced in some countries when driving a car. The original idea was to take no chances when a stranger came cantering towards you on the road. Whether a fight resulted or only a friendly shaking of hands, it was more convenient to have him within easy reach of your right hand.

In an arena where several riders are practicing at the same time regulations like that help to prevent unpleasantness. It is even better if everybody will ride in the same direction and change hands at the same time. In any case, those who are walking their horses, or working at a slower gait or tempo, should always stay inside the track. It is not regarded as good manners to pass a slower rider going in the same direction. A turn across the arena should be made instead, before getting so close to the other that his horse is disturbed.

Riders who have frequented bridle paths all know how it excites their horses if somebody comes tearing up from behind and passes without slowing down. Whether they are traveling in the same or in opposite directions, common courtesy demands that both slow to a walk or trot slowly by. If this rule is ignored when children are involved, the consequences may be bolting horses and serious accidents.

To follow a horse in front too closely is another bad habit that may lead to trouble, such as being kicked, for instance, or inflicting serious damage to a hind foot.

On the other hand, it is not advisable for a member of a group to be left too far behind. The result may be an un-called-for gallop, out of control. And the leader of a party may start a panic that he is powerless to stop if he changes to a faster gait too suddenly and without warning.

To sum up: Avoid doing anything that may disturb other riders or frighten their horses.

19. The Training of the Colt

The first schooling of a young horse decides his attitude toward human beings during the rest of his life. It will also permanently affect parts of his physic as well as his disposition and temperament. Lacking the ability to reason it is more difficult for him to correct the mistakes in guidance during childhood than it is for humans.

He is curious and eager and more than willing to learn, but he is not very intelligent. Much time and patience are necessary, but he will cooperate without difficulty as soon as he understands what is wanted of him. The use of force and punishment may "break" him, but some of his best qualities will always be destroyed in the process. Fear of people will become his prevailing characteristic. His instinct will be to resist, to balk, run away, or buck. Dull, lifeless resignation may also be the end product of stupid and brutal training methods. A few of them end up as "outlaws." The schooling of a young colt begins when he is a few weeks old. The way he behaves when the time comes to be saddled depends on how much he has been handled, petted and talked to during the first months of his life and whether his early experience with people has bred affection and trust or fear. He should learn to recognize his trainer's voice and the touch of his hand as a caress, to find pleasure in being groomed and having his feet picked up. Introduction to halter and snaffle bit is something new and interesting, nothing to be afraid of.

The first lesson in being guided involves only wise use of voice, a gentle hand and a halter. A long time is spent at the end of a longe before a saddle is put on his back, not to mention a rider. His adjustment to carrying the heavy weight must not be rushed, either, and lessons in understanding and obeying the aids should not be attempted until he is thoroughly familiar with walking and trotting under a rider.

The longe should be used extensively even after the schooling under saddle has begun. The longe is an important tool of the trade both for schooling and exercise, also in connection with the training of jumpers. Like everything else, it must be handled properly to be of real benefit.

The longe should be 25 to 30 feet long and made of

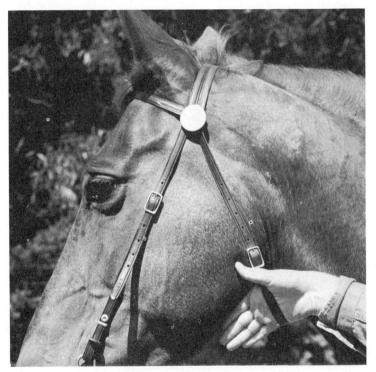

Throat Latch should never be tighter than this.

very flexible rope. A window sash cord is excellent. The
whip that goes with it should have a not too pliant
handle, be five to six feet long, and have a thong that
can reach the horse out on the circle. The longe is carried
in the left hand, neatly coiled to allow paying out more
line or pulling in slacks without getting entangled. At
the end of the line is a small ring attached to the middle
of a short leather strip with a buckle at each end to be
fastened to the rings of the snaffle bit. In order to simulate
the action of the reins, the ring at the end of the longe
has enough freedom to slide two or three inches toward
each end of the strap. If there is no such strap, the rope
must be knotted to both snaffle rings and changed every
time the horse changes hand on the circle. The longe
should never be tied to only one snaffle ring.

No longe equipment is complete without a surcingle,
padded to fit across the withers to prevent it from slipping.
The surcingle is provided with rings, placed so that the
horse's head can be kept in perpendicular position, slightly
flexed toward the center of the circle, by a pair of open
reins. This girth is an excellent preparation for the saddle.

A young colt's main interests in life are to eat and play.
The longer the trainer can preserve the illusion that he is
a friend and a playmate the better. Rough handling,
shouting and barking will scare him and make him nervous
and confused. In that condition he can not be expected
to be receptive to instruction and understand what is
wanted of him. All new equipment must be shown to
him and explained. Let him sniff at the rope and the
whip, convince him that they are not going to hurt him,
and be careful that they never do.

Until the colt learns to obey the longe and the whip,
the trainer should have an assistant, who will walk beside
him and lead him around the circle. The assistant gradually moves away from him with the whip pointed toward
him as a command to keep walking on the track. Both

trainer and assistant should face in the direction the colt is moving.

As part of the preliminary discipline that is the purpose of the longeing, the colt should, for instance, learn to stop when the trainer and his assistant turn to face him and walk toward them when told to do so.

Until the colt has become familiar with the bit, the longe should be attached to an ordinary halter, which later can be combined with a "watering snaffle." This contraption is a regular snaffle bit. A cross bar on each side is connected with the snaffle rings by short chain links or leather straps. In teaching the colt to accept the bit, the watering snaffle is fastened to the halter by the cross bar on the right side. The bit is then eased between the teeth and the left cross bar attached to the halter. By this simplified method a frightening struggle can be avoided.

As soon as the colt accepts the watering snaffle without fuss, it can be replaced by a regular bridle. Regardless of whether it may clash with local traditions and fads, the only type of bit that should be used is a snaffle. A curb will be added later but is taboo at this stage, and should be at any time if used alone.

This is also the time to put on the previously described surcingle and attach the open reins. They are left loose to begin with and shortened gradually until the colt becomes aware of their pull and the position of his head can be regulated. After a few lessons a light-weight saddle can take the place of the surcingle and the guide reins fastened to the girth with a flat knot. Extreme care must be taken in tightening both the surcingle and the girth of the saddle. The stirrups should be removed before the attempt is made to put the saddle on, and if the animal is high-strung and nervous, it is advisable to use a saddle blanket to start with. Make it a rule to begin all operations in front of the colt and give him an opportunity to watch what is going on and smell unfamiliar objects. Keep talk-

ing to him in a quiet voice all the time and interrupt
proceedings occasionally by picking up his feet.

The colt should learn to understand and obey words
like "walk," "trot" and "halt," always to be accompanied
by signals with longe and whip, corresponding to the action of reins and boots. The whip in the hands of the assistant trainer must never become anything but a guide

Picture shows two reins in each hand on both sides of ring
finger, snaffle on the outside. Used for jumping and cross-
country. For everyday riding and dressage work three reins
in the left hand, right snaffle in the right hand is preferable.
The two curb reins then are one on each side of the left ring
finger, the left snaffle rein on the outside of the left little
finger. The right snaffle rein held in the right hand runs
between little finger and ring finger. This grip on the reins
makes it easier to adjust them and prevents the curb reins
from becoming too tight. The technique of all four reins in
the left hand is used only on formal occasions. The right
snaffle then goes between the left ring finger and the index
finger; the other three remain as described above. All reins
run up through the hand and, on top of each other, are
locked in place by the thumb.

to be respected—not feared. Its correct use plays an important part in training and deserves more attention than it usually receives.

The more severe lessons in discipline, like longeing, should wait until the colt is well past two years of age so that they can be followed, without break in the schooling, by work under saddle.

A young horse should never carry weight until he has passed his third birthday and his bones are set. Up to that age they are soft and easily damaged. This is the reason why so many thoroughbred colts are crippled before they reach the ripe old age of 36 months. They are often put to work under saddle on the race tracks when they are 18.

The spine itself is in danger if a young horse is made to carry weight before he is ready for it. The neural spines stick up from the vertebrae like a row of fingers. The back muscles are fastened to them and normally they are well apart. A weight, too heavy for undeveloped muscles, will make the back sag; the neurals will touch and rub against each other. Sometimes they grow together and become a constant source of agony.

During my years in the cavalry we had a specially constructed "remount saddle" that was used during the first few months of training. It was very light and heavily padded. With the exception of a reinforced pommel, it had no wood or metal frame. Thick, padded rolls and knee cushions in front and similar protection across the cantle kept the rider's seat and thighs in a fixed position, close to the withers, while thick padding protected the horse's back.

The unchanging stability of the rider's seat is of the utmost importance. The immediate problem of the young horse, suddenly hampered by a heavy burden, is to regain his own balance, and it helps him a great deal if the load is stationary. I am aware of the fact that special saddles of this type are now rarely available and that trainers have to make do with what they have. The next best type of saddle is an English model with a short seat—a dressage saddle. The medieval monsters weighing 40 pounds or more are senseless, but unfortunately still in use. A training saddle should at least be light.

The initial steps of mounting a young horse are perhaps the most important among all the details that must be observed during the training process. Carelessness and stupidity, not to mention worse things, have ruined good horses without number and will no doubt cripple and spoil many more. I can only hope that there still are a few people around who "can be bothered" with a few tiresome words of common sense.

When mounting the first few times, the trainer should have two assistants, one to hold the horse and one to give him a leg up. The trainer stands close to the shoulder, well forward, with his left hand on the withers and his right on the saddle. He then bends his left knee, at the same time tensing the muscles in the leg. The assistant takes his ankle in both hands and eases him up gently, until he hangs on his stomach across the withers. This movement is repeated several times before he swings his right leg over and settles down in the saddle so lightly that the landing of a bird is a clumsy crash in comparison. After having the assistant lead the horse around for a minute or two, the rider dismounts and repeats the performance, being careful to insert his feet in the stirrups quickly as soon as his seat is in the saddle. When the time comes to mount without assistance, an assistant should help prevent the saddle from slipping by leaning on the stirrups on the off side.

During the entire period of training the trainer should never forget to reward his pupil for good behavior. There should always be a bucket of oats or some carrots handy, but never any sugar.

With the trainer in the saddle the young horse will at

first hesitate to start walking. This must not be mistaken for balkiness; he is just trying to adjust his balance and should not be disturbed, much less punished. Led by an assistant he should be allowed to take his own time, with frequent stops, until he has gained enough confidence to step out more freely. He should then begin to pay more attention to the rider and learn to respond to the clucking of the tongue accompanied by light pressures by the legs. Voice is still better than the use of the aids in guiding him. Several hours should be allowed for undisturbed moving straight ahead at a walk and trot. To let him follow behind an older horse always helps to get over the first difficulties.

The next step during the long months of schooling is to introduce him to the aids and teach him to obey them. Response to seat and weight comes naturally. Careful attention to correct distribution of pressure on his back makes it easier for the horse to understand what is wanted of him. Boots and bit should not take action for a change of direction, tempo or gait until the rider's weight is in the right position. It is more than ever necessary that the aids are "alive." A young horse is extremely sensitive, the mouth in particular, and the "life" in the bit and boots must be gentle, just enough to attract his attention without irritating. On the other hand, a pressure with the boots or a dead pull on the reins may have no effect. Providing the trainer understands the purpose of a whip and knows how to use it, he should always carry one long enough to reach behind his leg without disturbing the position of the hands. On trained horses the whip is used on the shoulder; on a trainee it can be useful as an introduction to the boot action and to make the horse conscious of the contact of the boot.

The reins must not become active at a too early stage. The main object is to allow the horse time to get used to the bit without being hurt or disturbed. When the more active use of the reins begins, it is advisable to deviate somewhat from the normal technique, in order to make the intention more obvious and to avoid roughness and force. When practicing a turn, for instance, the inside hand may be carried out sideways, giving the pull on the direct rein a kind of transverse effect, while the indirect rein steadies the head.

Flexing of the neck, as previously explained, is important. It should be practiced consistently as soon as training begins and never again be neglected. The flexing right behind the jaw both in the horizontal and the vertical plane is best done dismounted with a young horse. The observance of this detail will mean a horse that later in life remains pleasantly light in the hand and easy to control (at least until phony horsemen by strong-arm jerks and pulls have stiffened his neck and killed all feel in his mouth).

If the training is to be done right, it can not be done in a hurry. It will take from six to 12 months, and there are no short cuts.

20. The Tools of the Trade

Civilization has made impressive progress the last two to three hundred years. The wheel has been invented, carriages have been equipped with springs, people no longer eat with their fingers, at least not at formal dinners. There is even a movement to put pants on domestic animals, while the ladies are agitating energetically to shed what little covers they have left. Mankind is working overtime to improve everything. Except itself. Last year's models are discarded.

The horse business is an exception and presents a confusing picture. Some equipment, well known to the knights of the Crusades, is still in use, while better ways to handle a horse under saddle, laboriously developed for a couple of hundred years, are rejected with contempt and a decline toward the primitive is clearly indicated.

Better equipment is of small consolation to the horse as long as the rider does not know how to use it. An ignorant rider will turn anything into an instrument of torture. When primitive tools join forces with a primitive handler, the consequences are not pleasant to contemplate. But this is unfortunately the way the situation looks in many places today, and conditions are certainly not improving in spite of attempts to replace old models of various equipment with new and more humane things. The old model stock saddle and bridle—and all the regalia that goes with it—is still dear to the heart of the weekend cowboy, influenced from boyhood by Western lore—Hollywood style. Even if he realizes the advantages of a saddle better suited for his purpose, he can not bring himself to part with his romantically glamorous outfit.

The shape and form of the horseman's equipment in the less refined past had a double purpose: the rider's comfort and his ability to enforce his will by the use of mechanical contraptions. In this day and age, skill is supposed to replace force and the rider's comfort to be of little or no importance. A new element is appearing and taking form in relation to the treatment of animals: the humane considerations. Analyzing the effect of various kinds of equipment on the horse, let us take a look at the most vulnerable parts of his anatomy.

SADDLES

The back is obviously one of them since it has to support the combined weight of rider and saddle. The length and shape of the back varies. There are short backs caused by sloping shoulders; there are the long backs of the draft horse type that will have a tendency to sag because of sloppy, ignorant or indifferent riders. Trainers are frequently also neglecting the development and strengthening of the back muscles of young horses.

Regardless of its relative length, the part of the back immediately in front of the croup is weaker than the continuation of the withers. Besides, the kidneys are located under the small of the horse's back. A pressure, not to mention a pounding, on this delicate organ over a prolonged period of time will have disastrous consequences.

The saddle should be constructed to fit the conformation of the horse's back, allowing the weight to be evenly distributed over the limited area indicated by the animal's anatomical construction. Regardless of the shape of the horse's back, this area is as far forward as the withers and the free movement of the shoulders will permit. A good saddle should permit only a very limited shift of the rider's weight back and forth. The details of its construction should, however, be adjusted according to its purpose.

The "Mexican" Saddle. Built for working cowboys. Unsuitable for sports and pleasure riding.

Saddles built for cross-country riding or jumping usually have a longer seat than the school or "park" model and should not be allowed to be used by beginners.

The remount saddle used by the cavalry for the training and schooling is a good illustration of the general principles. It was heavily padded underneath and required no blanket. It had thick padded rolls both in front and rear that prevented both seat and thighs from sliding a single inch backward or forward.

A saddle blanket or a felt pad is an important part of any saddle and can do more damage than the saddle itself if the blanket is dirty or carelessly folded. A felt pad is even worse if it is allowed to become hard and crusty from accumulated sweat. This can be the reason for one of the most common forms of abuse, particularly among rent horses at public stables: saddle sores. They appear on the withers, under the cantle, or they are produced by the

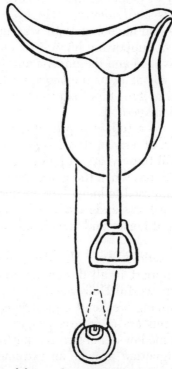

The Flat Saddle. Meant for sports and pleasure riding. Flat saddles constructed specially for dressage work have slightly shorter and deeper seats. Jumping and cross country model has a somewhat longer seat.

girth. Most of them are caused by poor equipment or badly adjusted saddles, blankets, or girths. But they can also be the result of the Sunday rider's antics. He will have a tendency to sit too far back because he just naturally slides in that direction. After a while he also becomes increasingly concerned about his lack of comfort. There are muscles here and there that begin to ache. Judging by painful sensations in his two seat knuckles, the saddle padding must be getting defective. At any rate, he starts to experiment with ways and means to relieve his misery. He moves backwards and sideways. He has even been observed trying to find anchorage half way up the cantle or hanging sideways, supporting himself on one thigh. When acrobatics of this kind and the nonchalant flopping around (which is the trade mark of the showoff) have been kept up long enough, nothing less than the hide of an elephant can remain undamaged.

The Western stock saddle is probably God's gift to the working cowboy, otherwise it is hard to understand why it has survived all these years. It gives him the support he needs in all directions when the going gets rough. Besides, he is not only supposed to know how to ride, but also how to take care of his horse and save him from being hurt. He also has a string of horses and can change to a new mount when necessary.

The western saddle gives the drugstore cowboy the badly needed support in all directions, too. This fact, in addition to the powerful Hollywood propaganda, explains its popularity among weekend equestrians and its amazing survival in this era of frantic progress.

Actually, this medieval monstrosity, particularly when it is used by the ignorant, can be an extremely efficient instrument of torture. Improvements in its original construction are now being made. But thousands of the old model are still in use. In fact, they appear to have even more romantic attractions than the glittering new ones. The old

type weighs up to 45 pounds. All this dead weight, added
to its primitive construction and the rider's mistakes must
classify it as a most undesirable type of saddle for sports
and recreation riding. It must be admitted, however, that
the stock saddle has a fascinating background.

When I was a boy, we had the skeleton of an old saddle
hanging in the corner of the tack room. Among other
things it had been dug out of a big Viking burial mound,
obviously the last resting place of an important chief. Naturally I was very interested in this relic and studied it
carefully; I can still recall the details of its construction.
When I was first introduced to the American stock saddle,
the similarity of certain features with the 500 to 600-year-
old remains struck me as obvious. There was for instance
the "horn," which was used by the mounted knights to
hang the reins on when they went into combat. Both
hands were busy with sword or lance and shield. The
"horn" is still there, for a different purpose. The obvious
explanation is that this type of saddle was brought to the
New World by the Conquistadors and passed on to the
horsemen of early America with few structural changes.
This same "horn" has in modern times found still another
practical use. The riders of the bridle trails find it very
handy to grab hold of in an emergency. However, of personal experience, I know of three cases of fatal accidents
caused by the "horn." In all three it pierced the rider's
chest when the horse fell and rolled on him. A flat saddle
might have meant survival.

The big, open stirrups are another death trap. It is easy,
particularly for a child's foot to slip through and get
caught. If you then fall off, you are hopelessly hung up
and dragged. Unlike the flat saddle, the old-fashioned
stock saddles have no safety lock that will allow the stirrup to come off under circumstances like this.

While the old stock saddle has been touted on the
screens day in and day out for so many years, no attention

has been paid to the saddle adopted by the U.S. Cavalry and named after General McClellan. From a horse's point of view, it is one of the best saddles ever built. It is light, it fits the back of any horse and it keeps the rider where he ought to be. Its weakness is that it is not sufficiently padded for the comfort of soft posteriors used to the cushion of an office chair. And then, of course, it has been neglected by the Madison Avenue experts while the stock saddle has become a kind of national symbol. It would certainly be a very long step in the right direction if public stables could be persuaded to replace what they have with McClellan saddles.

BITS AND BRIDLES

The mouth is the second important point of contact between the horse and its rider. Through the years "horse masters" have been well aware of this fact and taken full advantage of it. Their inventive genius has produced instruments of torture that in no way are inferior to those developed by the Spanish Inquisition or experts of the Gestapo. Only their purpose was somewhat different: control by force.

Most of those contraptions constructed for breaking and crushing have now disappeared from the scene, but enough of them still remain to make it too easy for sloppy and ignorant riders to draw blood, although many of them would obtain the same result with any kind of bit. Livery horses are still coming back from rides bleeding at the mouth or with their mouths so tender that they will shy away if you try to touch them.

Riding equipment, like everything else, has changed drastically through the centuries. Generally speaking, the tendency has been to make control possible without resorting to instruments of torture. Spurs started in the shape of needle sharp stilettos that could penetrate and

The double bit, snaffle and curb, properly adjusted and manipulated, is the best form for more advanced riding. The snaffle alone is ideal for beginners and for the schooling of the young horse.

lacerate the skin. Bits were constructed along principles of leverage that made it easy to break a jaw. Sometimes they were fortified with knife-like "spades" that would do a lot of damage and cause a lot of pain by a pull on the rein. But the horses certainly became "light in the hand" and would think twice before they tried to run away.

While progress may mean improvement in things mechanical, romantic traditions are unfortunately still interfering when riding equipment is concerned, at least in some localities where the popular image of dashing horsemanship is closely connected with violent action. Fine horsemanship makes no impression on the general public, because it is not spectacular and picturesque. The half-rearing, wild-eyed horse with the flying mane, the open mouth and the nose pointed to the sky is universally admired. What really is taking place is a performance illustrating the mistreatment of a gentle old horse, struggling frantically to escape a vicious attack of brutal spurs and bit.

21. There Still Are a Few

When I first met Hank he was in charge of the National Guard cavalry regiment's stables outside Dallas. I got to know him well. His horses, stables and equipment were in the kind of shape they should be. Not because Hank was a soldier. He was and is a horseman. At that time he was a cavalry sergeant. He used to be a cowboy (of the real, working kind) and had spent all his life in the saddle on the endless Texas plains. He could never be comfortable and relaxed sitting on anything but a saddle.

After the war Hank came to Southern California, where he now has a boarding and training stable. Young people also come to him to learn about horse husbandry and how to ride. Last year I went down to pay him a visit, talk about the years in Texas and maybe pick up something to write about. His wide grin was the same, and after exchanging a few insults referring to my waistline, in return for some rude compliments I still remembered as being regarded as fighting words back in Texas, he took me for an inspection tour around his establishment.

The first thing that struck me was the cleanliness inside and out. The spacious front yard was swept; stables, outbuildings and fences were white and looked like they had been painted recently. The regulation size school ring had a generous cover of sawdust that would not leave spots on the most elegant breeches in an emergency landing. There was a stable for 50 horses and it was, like the rest, immaculate and so free of unpleasant stench that I offended Hank by asking if he used boudoir deodorant. The aisles were scrubbed and still pleasantly damp from the morning scrubbing. The straw in the stalls had obviously been put there that morning; it did not just cover and hide a rank and rotting old pad underneath because here and there the clean planking showed.

Hank looked and acted too smug for his own good as I redoubled my efforts to find something that could be used to take him down a peg or two, with no success.

The tack room smelled refreshingly of leather and saddle soap instead of the sour and musty old sweat and rot that had become all too familiar. I could dig nothing objectionable out of the darkest corners. Everything made of leather left no doubt where the aroma of saddle soap originated. Saddle pads and blankets were clean and soft and hardly showed any traces of having been used. Bits and stirrups shone like silver. I began to understand why every horse around the place looked so happy and healthy and I could not help paying a silent tribute to the old cavalry's way of doing things. Amateur horsemen, not to mention commercial stables, pay no more attention to such matters than they have to. Felts and blankets used under the saddle are rarely cleaned until they are so stiff with dirt and dried sweat that they leave raw and bleeding sores on horses' backs. Filthy bits are excellent breeding grounds for bacteria and there is no better place for them to thrive than the mouth of a horse, particularly if it has been mutilated by primitive bits in brutal hands.

Grooming equipment was not neglected either. There were curry combs and brushes for every purpose. Most of the boarders had their own private toilet sets, and some of the owners had made it a habit to drop by and groom their own horses, but only after being thoroughly drilled in the proper cavalry technique. In fact, I had just watched one young lady giving her horse "the works" outside, with a curry comb in her left hand and a stiff, short-haired brush in the right, manipulating them with the vigor and rhythm of an old dragoon. She was busy on the back and flank at the time, applying the brush in long

strokes, first from rear to front, then immediately in the
opposite direction, smoothing the hairs ruffled with the
first stroke. The swing of the arm continued back for a
quick swipe of the brush over the curry comb in her left
hand to clean it for the next stroke. This steady one-two-
three rhythm was strictly according to the old cavalry
manual, and I can think of no better type of calisthenics
for young ladies who are concerned about their figures.

If the horse is very dirty, a curry comb should be used
as the first step of the grooming process to loosen up mat-
ted hairs on neck, back, flanks and thighs. For the boney
parts, the head, and lower legs, softer brushes are necessary, and a soft cloth should be used to clean the head,
not forgetting nostrils and mouth.

Combing of mane and tail comes next, and then finally
care of the feet. Every grooming kit should contain a pick
for this important part of a horse's toilet and also a special
knife—used by horseshoers—to remove flakes from the frog.

The grooming of the feet is not complete without a
careful inspection of the hoof. Cracks, soft spots and signs
of rot, loose shoes, or need of new ones must be attended
to immediately. It is worth remembering in this connection, that the not uncommon ailment called "founder"
starts as a painful swelling of the tender tissues of the
foot. In advanced cases, the sole drops down below the
wall of the foot. At this stage there is no cure. If the
founder had been recognized for what it was at an earlier
stage, the horse could have been saved.

Outside again, Hank and I were admiring the girl, still
hard at work on her horse. She had one of his front feet
up between her knees this time and was busily digging
out dirt. I noticed that, while she was bending over with
her back to the horse's head, she was keeping a wary eye
over her shoulder. "She has learned from experience,"
said Hank. "A couple of weeks ago, she forgot that a pet

horse likes to nibble, and—well, for a few days she didn't
like to sit down on anything hard."

It is always wise never to stand right behind a horse,
and it is better to stay at his side as close to him as possible, for instance, when you have to pick up a hind foot.
Talk to him and pat him on the croup first. Then let your
hand slide firmly down the leg, while you lean against
his flank with your shoulder. Grip the fetlock and pull the
leg forward, while you slide in behind him and bend his
leg back until you have it firmly between your knees. In
that position, the worst that can happen to you is to be
catapulted head over heels. You can't be kicked.

Most of the horses in Hank's stable were boarders. Many
of the owners, he told me, had ample facilities for keeping
them at home but sense enough to realize that they were
better off in Hank's hands. Both feeding, grooming and
care in general is in danger of becoming more or less hap-
hazard as a family responsibility. A horse's well-being
depends on many things, generally ignored by amateur
owners. The right kind of feeding, particularly in relation
to exercise, is probably the most important. A hard-work-
ing horse needs more and richer food than an idle one.

Irregular periods of work complicate the diet problem,
and a family horse living at home seldom enjoys any regularity. Children may play with him and hang on his
back every day of the week. Then some adult will take
him for an all-day ride during weekends, and he is
hungry and thirsty when he comes back. The rider, who
is fond of animals, takes the bridle off and enjoys seeing
him bury his nose in the water trough and gulp down large
quantities to his heart's content. Then he may be given all
the oats he can stuff into himself, while his master smiles
with kindly satisfaction, never suspecting that he has just
done something with probable serious consequences in
the form of indigestion, colic and the like. Overfeeding is

just as dangerous as starving and much more common. Veterinarians who specialize in horses agree that they have more trouble with overfed horses than with any other ailment. Cases of that kind are also the most serious. They quite often lead to founder.

Horses can live and thrive on many strange kinds of food, but candy and cookies affectionately offered by children must be taboo if you have any regard for your horse's health.

Hank's domain included a considerable area of open fields, which were used for grazing during the winter and spring. There were two or three sections separated by fences and used in rotation. A well-prepared bridle path ran all around this pasture land, widened here and there to make room for a few easy obstacles. The purpose of the track was to make it possible to get the horses away from the confines of stable and school ring for their daily exercise. Boys and girls who could pass as able riders often came out before going to school to help out with this chore.

Feeding followed strict rules. A few of the horses even had their feeding schedule pinned to their stalls if deviations from the regular routine were necessary on account of ailments or exceptionally hard work. Standard regulations called for such things as watering before eating, although water should be available at all times. If a horse was warm, either coming in from a ride or because the weather was hot, some hay was put in the watering trough, forcing him to suck the water through it and slow down the intake. If no hay or straw is available, it helps to leave the bit (particularly a double bit, snaffle and curb) in his mouth while he drinks. Under no circumstances should a horse be allowed to drink or eat until his respiration is normal.

It is advisable not to feed for an hour or so after work, and although grain and hay can be served simultaneously, it is preferable to wait until at least half of the hay ration has been consumed before the grain is offered. Preceded by water, grain and hay should be fed to the horse three times a day.

A horse can not always be allowed to eat all the hay he wants, least of all following a method only too often seen where the family pet lives at home: a bale of hay is opened and nonchalantly left in the corral, or wherever he spends his idle hours, with an invitation to help himself. If he tramples it into the dirt and makes it unfit even for bedding, it is his hard luck.

The grain ration must be carefully regulated in conformity with the amount of work the horse is doing and his condition in general. Calories do not affect a horse differently just because he has four legs. He needs, for instance, less grain in warm weather than in a cold climate. Salt must be within easy reach at all times.

The proper feeding of horses requires more knowledge, experience and good judgment than any other class of livestock. Unfortunately, the horses are in general the poorest fed. This is mainly due to a great lack of knowledge concerning the basic principles of equine nutrition. It is not uncommon for two horsemen, under similar conditions, to secure widely varying results with their feeding programs. All researchers agree that good green grass seems to have something quite superior in nutritive value. Horses come into full bloom and put on weight after some time in a lush pasture. Too much hay or roughage causes labored breathing, lack of endurance and a pot belly.

Many of the new concentrates, on the other hand, are lacking in bulk and may produce colic, among other things.

An eye-witness story was published recently in Northern California, and appeared in four local papers, dealing with the troubled life of horses that are treated as "members of the family." It says in part:

A resident of a well-to-do district hereabouts complained to the Humane Society about a neighbor's backyard horse left unattended for days. The owner just didn't know or take time to see if the animal's blanket needed changing after a recent spring storm. One family bought a horse, penned it up in a small corral and fed it nothing but oats. The horse not only had insufficient exercise and protection from wind and rain, but was receiving a diet much too rich even for a race horse.

The "weekend" horse and the "backyard" horse belong to the same category. Many times they are fed only occasionally, and when they are fed, they may be dumped huge quantities of food which can cause illness or even death.

Often they are taken out of their stalls, pens or fields and given "a good run" on the false assumption, that this is good exercise for a horse.

I have met few professional horsemen in my life who understood horses and their needs, and was understood by them like my friend Hank. When I first knew him in Texas, I saw him on many occasions walk composedly up to a vicious or nervous horse (even an "outlaw"), rub his nose gently, pull his ears and talk to him in a low voice, as if he were sharing a secret with him. Then he would slide smoothly up into the saddle with no perceptible adjustment of the reins.

I remember one horse in particular, one of the best in the squadron, with a man in the saddle. There was only one trouble with him: he refused to submit to shoeing. Unless Hank did it personally, that is. Before Hank took over the job, they had to put Veronal in the drinking water, making him lay down and go to sleep. It was an awkward business to get the shoes on him laying down.

I had for some time half unconsciously been hearing clinking and clanking sounds that could only be produced by a horseshoer in action. On our way to the source of the racket Hank told me that a couple of boys who studied

animal husbandry came in off and on for on-the-spot instruction in horse lore, including how to put on shoes.
Some of his pupils in general horsemanship also took advantage of the opportunity to learn the art of shoeing.
Hank always kept rubbing in the fact that there was more
to horsemanship than a more or less doubtful ability to
hang on to the saddle.

Sure enough, we found two young men in a frenzy of
activity. One of them had a horse's hindleg locked between his knees trimming back the toe, which obviously
had been getting too long. He was doing this correctly
from the underside and seemed to be well aware of the
good horse shoer's rule number one: Shape the shoe to fit
the hoof; do not shape the hoof to fit the shoe, which
would mean damaging the protecting wall of the hoof
and lead to rot and serious damage. The other boy was
holding a horse shoe by a tong with long handles in a
small furnace with glowing coal until it was white hot
and throwing sparks like a fire cracker. As soon as the
iron was heated to his satisfaction and pliable, he carefully adjusted its shape on the anvil, stuck it in a bucket
of water to cool and passed it to his partner to try if it
fitted the hoof snugly. If it didn't, it was sent back to be
heated and hammered again for another minute adjustment. When the shoe finally was accepted as satisfactory,
the next delicate operation was nailing it on with such
accuracy that the nails safely missed the sensitive parts
of the hoof and came out through the wall at the right
spot. For this purpose horseshoe nails are shaped in such
a manner that they will not go straight into the hoof. Instead they are deflected into a curved path, safely avoiding the soft insides of the foot.

Shoeing a horse in such a way that the result becomes
a protection instead of a cause of lameness is an operation
that should not be left in unskilled hands. In addition to
the purely manual dexterity required, a horse shoer must

have a detailed knowledge of the anatomical construction of the foot as well as of the effect of a badly shaped hoof on pastern and fetlock. Very often the placing of the shoe must be a corrective measure to ease strains in the foot and leg resulting from too long toes and uneven support.

Hank regarded the care of the feet of such importance in the education of a horseman that he kept some mummy-fied lower legs of horses, including hoofs, for serious students to practice shoeing and shaping. They might never actually get to nailing a shoe on a live horse, but they should know how.

A horse is exposed to the more or less malevolent attention of almost 200 kinds of parasites—internal and external. The best protection against illness is good stable management, the proper kind of feeding and sanitary conditions. At an establishment like Hank's they also have sense enough to call the veterinarian before it is too late.

Damage done to a horse on the trail or even in the school ring or exhibition arena can, of course, be equally serious, particularly when competitions are involved. Hank even expected owners riding their own horses to treat them decently as long as they used his stable facilities.

Anybody who is charged with the care of horses should have a sound knowledge of first aid and know how to handle simple ailments. The teeth, for instance, can cause a horse a lot of pain and severely affect his chewing and feeding. It is quite usual that the upper molars develop jagged corners on the outside, and the lower molars do the same thing on the inside, a condition that can be very painful and interfere with masticating.

I noticed that Hank's medicine chest, among many other things, contained a contraption used by veterinarians to be introduced in the horse's mouth and open it wide by turning a screw. There were also a couple of files for the teeth.

On my visit to the tack room, I had noticed, besides the regular Western and English saddles, four McClellan saddles, formerly regulation equipment of the U.S. Cavalry. I asked Hank if he kept them for sentimental reasons, in memory of his years with the army, or if he actually had customers who used them. As it turned out, they were used for what he called "remount work," which means training young horses. Hank explained that he remembered me talking about the remount saddle used in Europe and realized that the regular Western saddle was much too heavy and clumsy and had a too open seat. A flat saddle was also far from satisfactory because it permitted too much deviation from the absolutely stabilized seat and position that are so important when a young horse is first introduced to the terrifying experience of having a man on his back. To make it possible for him to find his balance, the least the rider can do is to stay in one spot and avoid throwing his weight around.

The nearest Hank could get to the right kind of saddle was the McClellan. It is very light weight, has a short seat and both pommel and cantle are built up, forcing the rider to stay in one place. Although Hank himself still uses his old cowboy saddle, he regrets that this excellent American cavalry saddle failed to get the popularity enjoyed by the Western. But, he reflected, it has never been advertised and glamorized; besides, even though it is easy on the horse, it is too hard for the soft rumps of weekend horsemen.

One of the more unusual features of Hank's school of horsemanship was to train a horse and its owner together. He would encourage youngsters—and older people too— to buy young, green horses, before a professional trainer had a chance to whip the life out of them. If the ability of the owner permitted, he would then be the first person the horse ever had on his back. From then on they would proceed together, guided by Hank himself or his instructor in English technique. Judging by what I saw, the results of this system were highly satisfactory.

Every owner of horses should have at least some knowledge of first aid and be able to recognize the symptoms of the most common ailments of the horse. Although colic is nothing more serious than a pain in the abdomen, it still kills more horses than any other internal disease. When the horse shows unusual uneasiness in the stable or corral, paws the ground, looks back at his flanks, kicks at his abdomen, lays down and gets up nervously and perspires, he almost certainly has a case of colic, and the doctor should be called immediately. Parasites are a common cause of colic, and so are defective and spoiled food. Both overeating and starvation will cause colic, and the danger of feeding too soon after heavy work, or just before, can not be exaggerated.

All that can be done, before the veterinarian arrives, is to keep the horse quiet and see that he does not hurt himself. Some time when the vet is around, it is also an excellent idea to mention subjects like tetanus and distemper and find out how to recognize them and what to do until he can get there.

Wounds can be of endless variations. Generally they can be classified as superficial scrapes and scratches, like saddle sores, lacerations, with deep tissue damage, sharp cuts or punctures, caused by wire or nails. A fresh wound should be cleaned thoroughly with soap and water, carefully removing all dirt and foreign matter. If possible, the hair around the wound should be shaved or at least clipped off. Frequent use of water after the initial cleaning will slow the healing and should be avoided. Use clean gauze or cloth instead.

If bleeding can not be stopped with a pad of cloth held firmly in place with a tight bandage, it must be held by hand until the veterinarian arrives. Care must be taken not to hamper circulation by bandaging too tightly. Bandages protect deeper wounds from dirt and other irritants and will in some cases restrict movement in the affected area that might interfere with the healing process. They should be changed every two or three days and not be removed until protective tissue has grown strong enough to leave the wound uncovered. A leg must never be bandaged without a solid padding. Not so long ago, it was taken for granted that if a horse broke a leg, he was done for. Nowadays some fractures may not mean the end. Sometimes they can be repaired, but only if the victim can be immobilized until expert help arrives.

Inflammations and swellings, resulting from bruises or sprains, are treated with ice packs, cold water bandages, or running water from a garden hose. If a horse goes lame on the trail and water is available, let him stand in it for an hour or so.

Some care must be observed in the use of heat applications. They are meant to increase circulation and encourage and speed up the healing of tissues. Applied too early they may actually do a good deal of damage. Poultices and the mild heat of liniments also help to localize and draw wound infections to the surface.

When I was leaving, Hank summed up his credo: "I don't care what kind of saddles they ride in, or how they are dressed up. It is what they have inside their skulls that decide whether they are horsemen or not."

Hank had created a place, where everybody, except the phonies, were happy, the horses included.

22. Concluding Reflections

In spite of well-meant, but half-hearted efforts to save
saddle horses from abuse, it is only too obvious that they
still are the step children among domestic animals. Not
because they are not important. Quite the contrary, it appears to be their misfortune that they are so useful in so
many ways. The horse is so big and dumb and gentle and
patient that he easily becomes a defenseless victim in the
clumsy and incompetent hands that, with the help of
ropes, whips, murderous spurs and bits, try to shape him
into an instrument for the satisfaction of human greed,
prestige and pleasure.

Remember President Johnson playing with his dogs?
Their yelps were heard around the world and caused a
flood of protestations, both from individuals and from organizations, denouncing the heartlessness of the perpe-
trator.

We rarely, if ever, hear similar howls of indignation
when horses are involved. But, of course, they cannot
squeal or even look pathetic and appealing like a spoiled
pup in distress, even if they are suffering severe pain. The
symptoms may be noticeable only to experts. The public
is blinded by the glamor of the horseshows, the excitement
of the rodeos and the race tracks. All the same, there is
much going on right in front of our eyes that can only be
classified as abuse. The trouble is that we are so used to
some forms of mistreatment, that we take them for granted
and fail to recognize them for what they are. Of course,
if a horse is found with a bloody back, limping badly or so
starved that his ribs stick out, somebody will usually object and even try to do something about it. But what about

the family pet that looks square, instead of beautifully rounded, when seen from behind, and pants like a hunting dog if you trot him for 60 seconds? All members of the family are so fond of him that they stuff him with rich food, not to mention candy and cookies. Who would ever suspect that he probably is a very sick horse well on his way to being killed by affection?

It is a sad fact that the family pet horse rarely lives a life of Riley. If he is not exactly confined for living quarters to the backyard, where the family washing used to hang, his accommodations are frequently primitive and unsuited for his well-being.

A horse's mouth is very sensitive, at least before it has been brutalized so it has lost all feeling, and the naked gums have no protection from the bit. Nevertheless, there seems to be no objection to the common displays of horsemanship, both on the screen and even in parades, where violent jerks on the reins cause the horses to throw their heads up in desperate attempts to avoid the agony inflicted by the bit.

The rider may simply be ham-handed, but frequently his intention is to show off, to create the illusion of a fiery steed, controlled by the firm hand of a master. The less glamorous fact is usually that the steed is nothing more than a placid old nag, surprised and scared half to death by unmerited punishment. But the admiring audience accept the performance at face value. They do not realize that what they see is a gentle horse, tortured by a bit constructed for the purpose of inflicting pain, assisted by spurs having corresponding effect.

Every form of sport and athletics follows strict and detailed rules of technique. Equitation as practiced today is an exception, regardless of the fact that it is the most complicated of all, since a live animal is involved. Instead there is an endless confusion of conflicting theories and practices, invented and fanatically defended by self-styled experts. They all develop their own following—innocent beginners or social climbers who are influenced by considerations that have little relation to the care and understanding of horses. It is not surprising that intelligent youngsters laugh at the idea of taking riding lessons. I was recently invited to give a talk at a Horsemen's Association meeting, but was instructed not to touch the subject of equitation technique.

The most tragic consequence of conditions like this is perhaps the loss of the old horseman's knowledge of how to protect a horse from unnecessary suffering and abuse. When I went to school it was constantly impressed upon me never to swallow whole any piece of information or knowledge without trying to find out WHY it should be just so and WHY NOT a little bit different. This rule applied to academic matters in general and I cannot fathom WHY it should be ignored when the handling of such a high-class animal as the horse is the problem. Nevertheless it is regarded as bad manners to ask an expert on the subject "WHY."

I noticed an ad in the paper recently in which a real estate developer in a district where the possession of a horse is more important for social prestige than good table manners. In addition to commodities like swimming pools and landing pad for helicopters there would be a stable, complete with two live horses. Just plunk down a deposit, move in, and you are a horseman, among other things.

An incident in a cavalry officers' mess 50 years ago has stuck in my memory. The colonel was asked what he thought about the new lieutenant. "How should I know," retorted the colonel. "I haven't seen him ride yet." He was not referring to the newcomer's equestrian ability.

Appendix

The following are not pictures of circus stunts. They are official photographs taken at the French Cavalry School at Saumur and are intended to illustrate how a horse's many latent talents can be developed into spectacular performances in advanced dressage. Force is never used and to hurt a horse was a punishable offense in the cavalry of yesteryear.

A foursome of the famous "Cadre Noir," French Cavalry School, Saumur, France.

Drill team of the "Cadre Noir" riding a stately gavotte. Every rider and horse is in perfect form for collected performance, with seat, hands and boots in position for complete control.

A "Courbette."

Four stages of a High School dressage movement, the "Capriole."

a. Starting with a "Levade"

c. End of Flight

d. Landing

Glossary

Big Volte—Circle, completely filling one end of arena, touching one short side and both long sides (the "Parade Points")

Boot—Calf of the leg

Change Hands—Reverse direction by crossing arena from one long side to the other, by using a small volte or the diagonal of the arena

Direct Rein—A pull

Half Parade—Pulling in from faster to slower gait (not tempo)

Indirect Rein—Exerting pressure on the neck and shoulder in support of direct rein to enforce change of direction

Longe—Long, flexible rope, attached to the bit, trainer holding the other end, guiding the horse in a circle

Poleing—Rapping the horse's knees sharply with a pole while passing the jump

Riding Left Hand—Left side toward center

Riding Right Hand—Right side toward center

School Ring—Rectangular arena with the long sides two to three feet longer than twice the length of the short sides, permitting simultaneous use of both big voltes; corners of arena should be sharp, never rounded.

Small Volte—Circle, 15 to 25 feet in diameter, executed from one of the long sides of arena